HOW TO DRAW & PAINT IN OILS

CONTENTS

Oil

THERE ARE VARIOUS ways of undertaking the preparatory stages of an oil painting. Here the composition is roughly outlined using a soft pencil; this method requires a light touch as heavy pressure may dent the canvas and cause the stretched surface to sag. The composition is divided roughly in half, but the artist has taken care to avoid making a completely symmetrical division of the picture plane, as this would interfere with the spatial illusion.

The low wall and brightly lit garden urn on the left of the painting underline the horizontal emphasis but, more importantly, provide a focal point which contrasts with the large expanse of green. The result is to create an overall sense of harmony. The shades of green are varied by the addition of blue, white, yellow and red.

The texture of the surface was enlivened by spattering wet paint from the end of the brush and constantly altering the directions of the brushstrokes. The best way to apply the paint is to vary the techniques; for instance, lay thin glazes over patches of solid color, scrub the paint into the weave of the canvas, and feather the brushstrokes into textured trails.

Materials

Surface
Stretched, primed canvas

Size
39in × 30in (98cm × 75cm)

Tools
1in decorator's brush
Nos 6 and 8 hog bristle brushes
No 8 round sable brush
Wooden artist's palette

Colors

Black	Cobalt blue
Burnt sienna	Chrome green
Burnt umber	White
Cadmium red	Yellow ochre
Cadmium yellow	

Medium
Turpentine

1. Draw up the composition lightly in pencil. Block in a loose impression of the background shapes with thin paint. Use greens with blue, yellow and red.

2. Continue to develop the shapes, varying the tonal contrasts and breaking up the color masses with linear brushmarks and small patches of different hues.

3. Lay in a solid expanse of chrome green across the whole of the foreground, using a 1 in (2.5 cm) decorator's brush.

4. Work over the sky and around the forms of the trees with a thick layer of light blue. Draw back into the green shapes with the brush to make the outline more intricate.

5. Work over the colors with fine linear brushmarks and thin layers of dribbled and spattered paint to increase the variety of tone and texture.

6. Define the shape of the wall with small dabs of brown, red and pink laid against strong black shadows. Blend and soften the color with a dry brush.

7. Work over the whole image making slight adjustments to the shapes and colors. Bring up the light tones and darken shadows.

8. Brush in a thick layer of bright green over the right of the foreground, working into the dark shadow area to bring out the illusion of light and shade.

Details of wall · outlining the urn redefining tree outlines

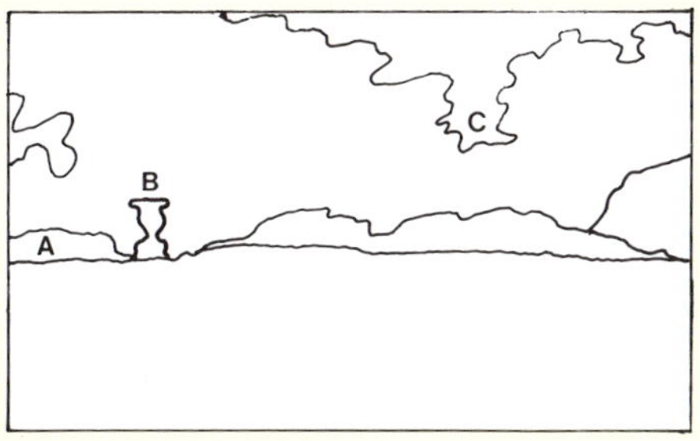

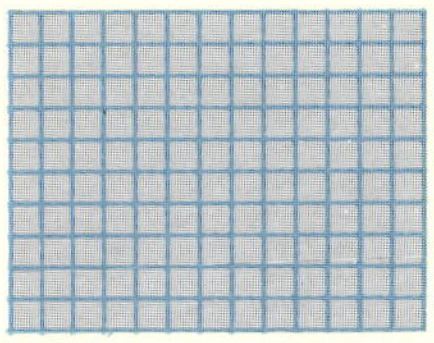

A. With a small sable brush, the artist is here putting in details in the wall. The previous layer was allowed to dry thoroughly before overpainting.

B. With a small bristle brush, the artist is here working carefully around the urn to strengthen outlines.

C. With a small sable brush and a thickish mixture of pale blue paint, the artist works back into the tree shapes.

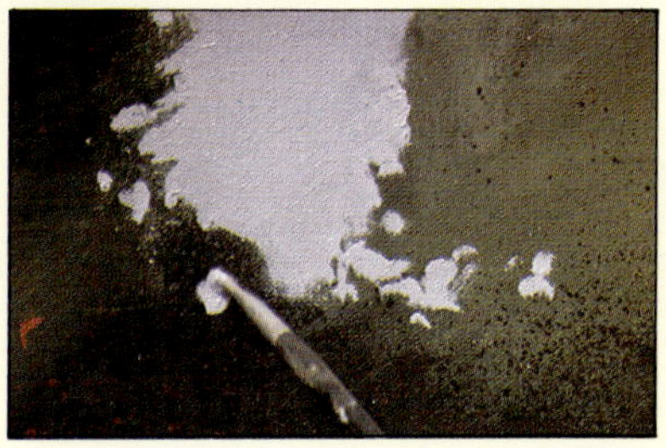

IN ALL PAINTING and drawing, the artist's decision on what media and techniques he or she uses to create a picture is a highly individual and selective process. The factors involved are a combination of practical skill, an understanding of the media and techniques and, most importantly, how the artist sees the picture in his or her mind's eye.

In this picture the *alla prima* method has been used. This is a quick, direct method of painting which can be used to create a bold and exciting picture in a short period of time. From a rough sketch, the artist works directly on to the surface, as opposed to the traditional method of building up layer upon layer of color, or working from dark to light. In unskilled hands, this sometimes can be risky as in laying down thick, heavy areas of paint, the artist is often simply hoping that the result will reflect the initial intention. When working as heavily as this, the main danger is of either building up the paint surface too quickly or mistakenly putting down wrong colors. However, one of the beauties of oil paint is that it can be easily scraped off and the artist can begin again.

To work with bold color requires a good color sense and a knowledge of how the individual colors interact with one another. Here, the artist has used 'unnatural' colors such as purples, greens, and reds over basic earth tones to both preserve the feeling of the subject and add interest and variety to the painting.

Materials

Surface
Prepared canvas board

Size
24in × 20in (60cm × 50cm)

Tools
Nos 2 and 4 flat bristle brushes
Palette
Palette knife
Rags or tissues
Willow charcoal

Colors

Burnt umber	Permanent magenta
Cadmium red light	Prussian blue
Cadmium yellow light	Raw sienna
Cadmium yellow	Raw umber
Cobalt blue	Yellow ochre
French ultramarine	White

Medium
Turpentine

1. After lightly sketching in the subject with willow charcoal, apply a thin wash of general color areas in cool and warm tones with a No 4 bristle brush.

2. With burnt sienna and cadmium yellow, overlay the roughed-in areas with thick, short strokes of color, using the stroke to define the shapes.

3. Build up the dark tones with Prussian blue and burnt umber and lighter 'dark' tones in green. Add touches of cadmium red as highlight areas.

4. Develop the light areas with cadmium yellow, ochre, red, and purple mixed from ultramarine blue and magenta. Develop water with Prussian blue.

5. Using a No 2 bristle brush, continue to lay in the water highlights in cadmium yellow and white, allowing the underpainting to show through.

Cloud texture · modelling rocks · water highlights

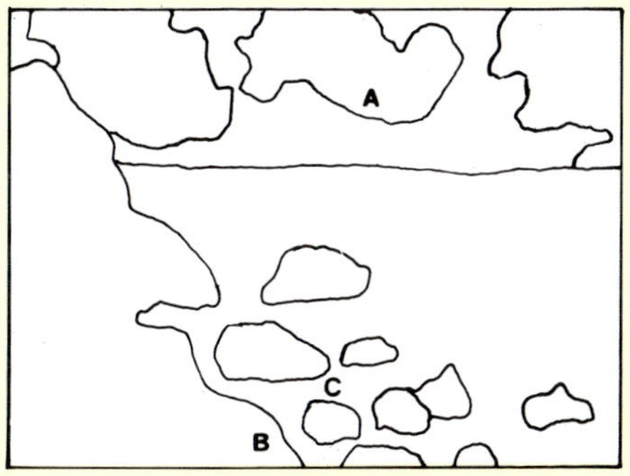

A. The artist is here putting in cloud shapes with a thick, opaque paint mixture and a small bristle brush.

B. Allowing colors to mix directly on the surface, the artist puts in thick strokes of paint in the rocks, allowing previous layers to show through.

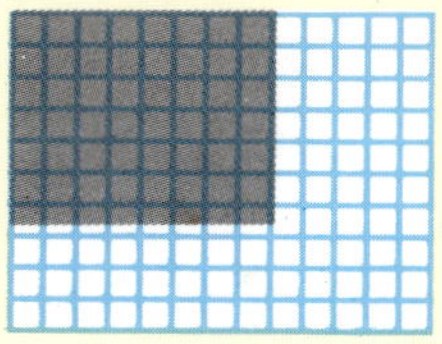

C. With a small bristle brush, various tones are touched into the water area to create a rippled texture.

THE MAIN TECHNIQUE demonstrated in this painting is considered particularly suitable for landscapes involving broad planes of color. The paint is applied thickly with a knife in simple shapes and, as a result, details emerge from the paint surface, rather than being dictated by the structure of the drawing. The composition is built up with overlaid layers of impasto paint giving a craggy, ridged texture. Each individual shape has a ragged edge where small vestiges of previous layers break through the top coat of color. In the final stages the work is coated with very thin, liquid glazes of color. These settle into the pitted impasto to form a veined sheen over the surface, drawing the tones together.

The limited range of color serves to focus attention on the texture of the paint, as does the simplicity of the composition. The balance of tone, color and texture is achieved by continual adjustment of the paint mixtures. The technique must be carefully controlled because the paint is thick and wet – frequent drying out periods may be needed before further layers can be added. Use palette knives to lay in thick paint areas and spread glazes with a clean rag to work the color into the surface.

Materials

Surface
Stretched, primed canvas

Size
12in × 9in (30cm × 22.5cm)

Tools
Palette knives: short trowel, 3in (7.5cm) cranked blade, 3in (7.5cm) straight blade; palette; rags or tissues

Colors

Paint:	*Pastels:*
Alizarin crimson	Black
Black	Cerulean blue
Cerulean blue	Ultramarine blue
Payne's grey	Yellow ochre
Prussian blue	
White	

Mediums
Linseed oil
Turpentine

1. Lay a wash of thin grey oil paint over the whole canvas, rubbing it in with a clean rag. Draw up the basic lines of the composition with oil pastels.

2. Apply thick layers of paint with a palette knife, blocking in the shapes with light blues, grey and mauve.

3. Still using the palette knife, build up the textured surface, lightening the tones of the colors. Work in broad, directional sweeps of broken color.

4. Continue to lay in grey and blue tones, varying the direction of the strokes.

5. Heighten the colors, working over the central shapes with solid white and light greys. Allow the underlayers to show through the thick paint.

6. Adjust the tones over the whole work to warm up the color balance. Even out the colors but keep the thick impasto quality.

Underpainting · painting with palette knife

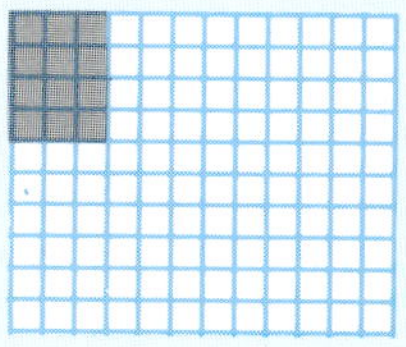

The artist blocks in general color areas with a palette knife, using a thick, opaque mixture of paint.

A thin ground of grey paint and turpentine has been rubbed into the canvas. On top of this the artist puts in the general outlines of the composition in oil pastel.

Draw the knife across the surface, blending the paint well into the canvas with even consistent strokes.

MANY ARTISTS FIND that working from photographs is an acceptable way of creating landscapes. However, there are disadvantages. Although the method enables an artist to increase his or her range of subject matter, it is limiting in terms of a fixed viewpoint and static lighting. The artist can compensate for this by exploiting colors and textures of the painting and by developing aspects of the image which naturally attract attention.

In this painting, the warm glow of light and pattern of trees and flowers have been exaggerated and used as the basis for a more colorful interpretation of the subject. The bright pastel colors of the sky are echoed in the pathway through the center of the picture, while the predominance of green has been enlivened by adding red, forming a contrast of complementary colors.

You can experiment with brushwork, laying the paint on quite thickly; oil paint can be scraped off and the surface reworked if an area of the painting is unsuccessful. Use three or four different brush shapes and sizes and vary the strokes between the tip and flat of the bristles. If necessary, let the painting dry out for a few days before completing the final stages, so that clear colors and clean whites can be laid over the darker tones.

Materials

Surface
Prepared canvas board

Size
24in × 20in (60cm × 50cm)

Tools
2B pencil
Nos 3 and 5 flat bristle brushes
No 1 round bristle brush
No 4 filbert bristle brush
Palette

Colors

Alizarin crimson	Cobalt blue
Black	Hooker's green
Cadmium green	Terre verte
Cadmium red	Ultramarine blue
Cadmium yellow	Violet
Chrome orange	White

Medium
Turpentine

1. After sketching in the composition, with a very thin wash of green and turpentine, quickly block in main shapes with a large, soft sable brush.

2. Load a bristle brush with cadmium green well thinned with turpentine and scrub in the basic composition, working with black and yellow.

3. Thicken the paint and lighten the tone of the colors, adding cobalt blue and violet to the palette. Work quickly over the painting with broad brushstrokes.

4. Develop the tonal contrast by drawing into the image with black and increasing the range of warm, light colors and mid-toned greens.

Highlighting · blocking in shapes

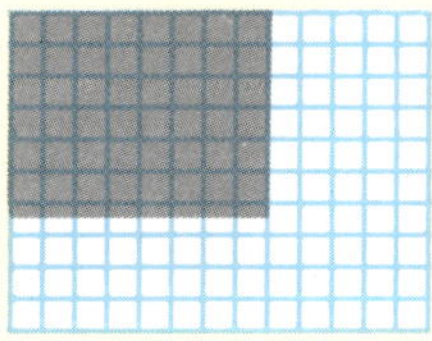

With a large bristle brush, the artist blocks in rough shapes of pale blue in the stream with thickish paint.

5. Work into the shapes of the trees with red and black and block in thick slabs of green, building up the texture by varying the quality of the brushmarks.

6. Use the point of a fine, round bristle brush to develop the linear structure of the composition and to color details. Paint in dark tones with ultramarine.

7. Elaborate the texture in the foreground with finely crosshatched brushstrokes of red, green and yellow woven across the previous work.

8. Give form and density to the foreground area with streaks and dabs of color. Add depth in the shadows with dark red and blue contrasted with white patterning.

After drawing in the tree outlines in green, the artist is here working into the white areas between with a pale pink.

ONE HUNDRED YEARS ago, few artists would consider doing a landscape painting from anything other than the actual subject, *plein air* painting being synonymous with the great artists of the day. Today however, painting out of doors has become something of an anomaly and the artist is often looked upon as an object of curiosity. Most landscape painters learn through experience what is required to adapt themselves and their work to working out of doors. Choose your materials and equipment carefully and plan to be working under poor rather than perfect weather conditions. Do not bring a lot of materials with you; the fewer the better.

In this painting, the artist has purposely chosen a view with an interesting combination of colors and textures. The neutral, earth tones of the buildings work well with the leafy green forms of the trees, the touches of red and yellow are just strong enough to enliven general color areas.

A good point to keep in mind is that when working closely from the subject, it is not necessary to paint or draw exactly what you see before you. In this case the artist has chosen certain objects, shapes, and colors and used them to the advantage of the painting, sometimes exaggerating and sometimes underplaying colors and shapes to make the picture work as a harmonious unit.

Materials

Surface
Card sized with rabbit skin glue

Size
11.5in × 9in (29cm × 22.5cm)

Tools
No 3 bristle brush
Palette

Colors

Aureolin	Chrome green,
Black	Cobalt blue
Cadmium red light	Raw umber
Cadmium red medium	White
Cadmium yellow medium	Yellow ochre

Medium
Linseed oil
Turpentine

1. Working from the center outward, draw in general subject outlines in pale blue with a No 3 bristle brush and begin to apply a thin raw umber tone.

2. Carry this same color outward from the center. Keep the paint consistency thin and work loosely.

Touches of color · scratching back

Above: Bright touches of color will often enliven an otherwise monochromatic painting. In this painting, the small red flag shapes add a valuable touch of interest to the finished picture. Right: By scratching back through the wet paint with the end of a brush, an interesting texture can be obtained.

3. Put in basic horizontals and verticals in the blue used for the initial sketch. Carry green and brown tones over the painting. With cadmium red put in the flag shapes.

4. Mix chrome green, cadmium yellow and white. Thin with turpentine and loosely work in the foreground trees.

5. Continue over the painting developing lights and darks. Work back into previously painted areas and develop details.

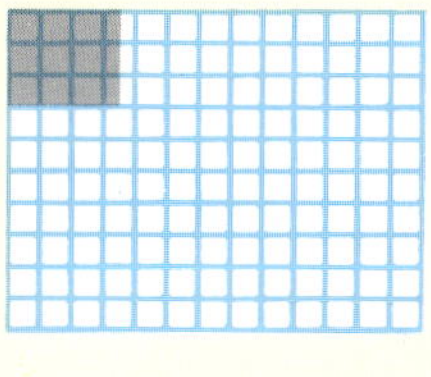

WHETHER PAINTING OR drawing, few artists will work on a picture as a group of individual and independent parts. An artist will rarely begin in one corner and progress across the page, or complete a section without regard for the rest of the picture. There is sound reasoning behind this. While the artist may have a good idea of what the finished picture is to look like, it is impossible to predict exactly the result of each brushstroke and how it will affect the picture as a whole. There is a natural rhythm to painting which involves a constant checking and re-checking of the work – not only in a particular area, but in all areas simultaneously. As small and insignificant as one brushstroke may seem, it is impossible to put down a touch of color without it affecting every other color.

In studying the progression of the work shown here, the rhythm of work becomes clear. The artist mixes a color, applies a few touches, and with that same color moves to another part of the painting. The sky color is used not only in the sky, but in the trees and water as well. The purplish tone used as an underpainting is repeated throughout the painting in various shades and tones.

This is an efficient way of painting as it saves the artist from having to mix and match colors each time they are needed. More importantly, this method gives the picture unity which is not overt or obvious to the viewer. It is also the wisdom behind using a few colors and from those mixing other colors and tones. By limiting the palette to three or four colors, the artist is automatically ensuring that the painting will have harmony.

Materials

Surface
Prepared canvas board

Size
18in × 24in (45cm × 60cm)

Tools
Willow charcoal
Nos 2, 4 flat bristle brushes
Palette knives
Palette

Colors

Alizarin crimson	Cerulean blue
Cadmium red medium	Viridian
Cadmium yellow medium	White

Medium
Turpentine

1. Very lightly rough in the subject with willow charcoal. Block in the general color areas with a No 4 brush using tones of chrome green and violet.

2. With pure cerulean blue and a lighter shade of this (add white), put in water and tree highlights. Use cadmium yellow medium to describe the lighter tones.

3. With a No 2 brush, mix viridian green and white and develop the tree on the right using short, directional strokes.

4. Mix alizarin crimson and cadmium red medium and put touches in the green of the trees. Add white to this mixture and put in water highlights.

5. Lighten the blue-green shade used in the tree by adding white and carry this over into the water area. Lighten this mixture and block in the cloud shapes.

6. With a No 2 brush, mix cadmium yellow light and white and put in the sky tone. Carry this into the water, defining tree and sky reflections.

Overpainting · strengthening shapes

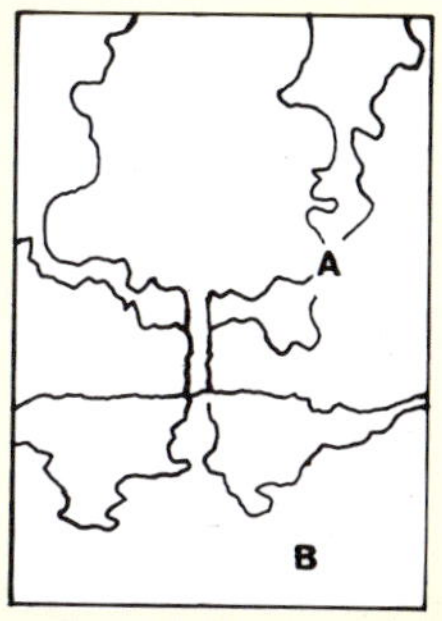

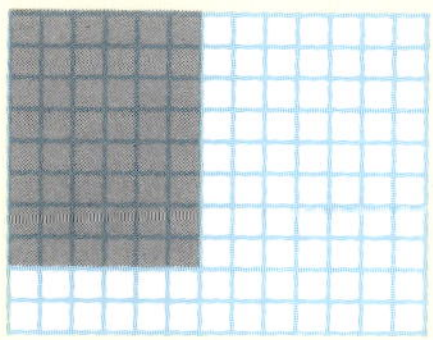

A. To strengthen the contrast between the tree outlines and the sky, the artist is here working with cadmium yellow and a small brush, working around tree shapes.

B. Overlaying the thin underpainting of the shadow areas in the water, the artist lays in short strokes of thick, undiluted paint.

Oil

WHILE THE ARTIST may use a natural history subject to successfully capture the essential characteristics of the subject, it may also be used as a vehicle for creating a dramatic picture.

In this painting, the background colors are part of the range used to paint the animals. Although this provides a close harmony in the whole image, the tones must be handled carefully, or the figures will merge into the background. The dark colors of the animals are a rich texture compared with the solid black behind. The flat pink color of the floor is modified and enlivened with a pattern of shadowy color.

Oil paint is a particularly suitable medium for this subject, as it can be blended and streaked to create an impression of soft fur. It is important to study the color carefully. Dark brown fur will have tints and lights which can be used to enrich the painting.

As a starting point, sketch out the forms loosely with a broad bristle brush but allow the overall shapes to emerge gradually in patches of color, treating each shape as a solid mass.

Materials

Surface
9oz cotton duck stretched and primed

Size
30in × 30in (75cm × 75cm)

Tools
Nos 3 and 6 flat bristle brushes
No 8 round sable brush
1in (2.5cm) decorators' brush
Wooden studio palette
1in (2.5cm) masking tape

Colors

Black	Cadmium yellow
Burnt sienna	Cobalt blue
Burnt umber	Raw sienna
Cadmium red	White

Medium
Turpentine

1. Draw up the outline of the animal with a dark brown mixed from raw umber and black. Use a bristle brush and work freely to lay in the shapes.

2. Start to work into the head, sketching in the features with the tip of the brush and blocking in the colors of skin and fur.

Working from sketch · blocking in tones · face details

When painting or drawing animals, it is usually easier for the artist to make rough sketches from the live subject which are later used as reference for the finished work. Here the artist is working from a sketch pad.

After the artist has roughed in the general shapes and positions of the animals, he begins to develop the faces. Using a large brush and color mixtures thinned with turpentine, he blocks in general color areas, scrubbing the paint into the surface and allowing these tones to blend with the black underpainting.

3. Use a sable brush to build up detail, developing the tonal structure of the head. Block in the whole shape of the body loosely with thin paint and a large brush.

4. Work up the color over the image with pinks and browns, strengthening the dark tones. Lay a thin layer of paint over the shape of the second animal.

5. Paint freely into both shapes, gradually improving the details of the form and at the same time intensifying the tonal contrasts. *(continued overleaf)*

Working over the damp underpainting, the artist begins to develop the details of the animal's face. Using a small sable brush and a thick paint mixture, he works over the initial black underpainting, darkening and refining. It is better to work over a damp surface as errors can be either scraped off or blended into the wet surface.

6. Fill in background color with a layer of thin paint. Use masking tape to make a straight line across the canvas and paint into the outlines to correct the shapes.

7. Dab in a multi-coloured texture over the plain area of floor, overlaying dots of red, pink, blue and yellow.

8. Scumble a thin layer of color over the patterning and thicken it gradually so that some areas of colored dots show through. Brush in solid black across background.

Spattering · putting in background

After the stippled background has been allowed to dry, the artist works with a decorators' brush, loosely blocking in color.

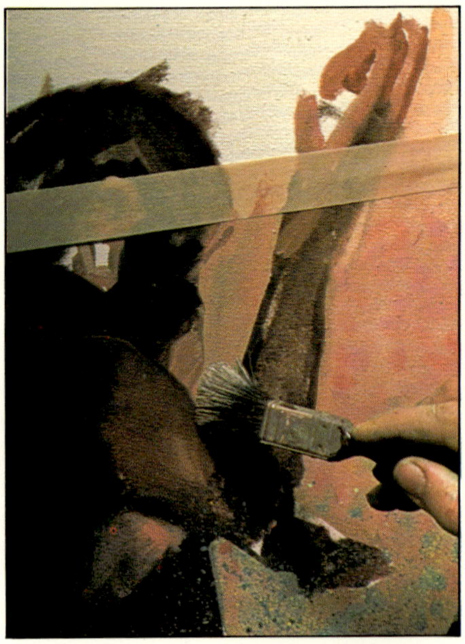

Right: An interesting paint texture can be created by spattering and stippling with a paint brush. The brush should be fairly large, stiff, and dry. The paint consistency is determined by the density of tone desired: the thicker the paint, the stronger the tone and larger the spatter. Above: The overall effect of the surface can be seen in detail. By overlaying a number of colors, from a distance the area will appear to blend into a continuous tone.

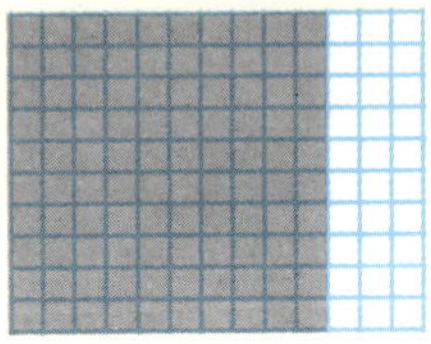

9. Draw back into the details of the face with a fine brush, adjusting the shapes and colors. Enrich the black and brown of the fur to give it texture and sheen.

10. Mask off the black background and work across with another layer of color to intensify the dark tone.

11. Draw up light brown shapes on the pink floor to suggest cast shadows. Finish off with white highlights in the fur.

TAKE TIME setting up a still life as the arrangement of the subject is entirely within your control. Move the objects around and consider the overall appearance from different viewpoints. Remember that the full freshness of flowers will not last long and natural light will change gradually during a day's work. Be prepared to work quickly and observe the subject extremely closely throughout the painting process.

Oil paint is the best medium for this type of subject. It keeps its true color as it dries, unlike watercolor which loses brilliance. It also mixes more subtly than acrylics so it is the most suitable medium to describe the range of vivid color and veiled, shadowy hues in the subject.

To establish the basic shapes and tones the composition is first drawn up in monochrome with layers of thin paint. The color is then built up gradually over the underpainting, initially modified by the tonal drawing and gaining full clarity in the final stages. Working quickly in oils means laying the paint wet-into-wet so brushmarks must be light but confident in order to apply colors directly without mixing them on the canvas. Thicken the paint slightly at each stage, adding gel medium where necessary. To make corrections, lift the paint carefully with a clean rag and rework the shapes. Check the drawing and color values continually as the painting evolves.

Materials

Surface
Prepared canvas board

Size
16in × 20in (40cm × 50cm)

Tools
Nos 3 and 6 flat bristle brushes
No 5 filbert
Sheet of glass or palette
Rags

Colors

Alizarin crimson	Permanent rose
Cadmium lemon	Prussian blue
Chrome oxide	Ultramarine blue
Chrome yellow	Vermilion
Cobalt blue	Viridian

Mediums
Rectified spirits of turpentine
Linseed oil
Gel medium

1. Use a flat bristle brush and cobalt blue paint to sketch in the basic lines of the composition. Thin the paint with turpentine and block in broad areas.

2. Strengthen dark tones with alizarin crimson, forming a purple cast over the blue. Draw into the pattern of shapes in more detail.

4. Work on the flowers, drawing in small shapes of red, pink and white. Vary the tone and density of the colors to suggest the form.

5. Refine the drawing with the tip of the brush and lay blocks of color with the bristles flat on the canvas.

7. Brighten the color of the leaves with light green, giving them more definition against the background. Lighten the table top with a layer of warm brown.

8. Brush over the background with a thin layer of blue mixed with a little red. Work over the blues in the foreground with a full range of light and dark tones.

3. Work into the foliage and jar with patches of green, mixing in touches of yellow and crimson. Paint in the background with brown and grey.

6. Bring up the tones of the white and pink flowers, applying the paint more thickly. Add details to the greens in the jar, mixing in yellow and white to vary the colors.

9. Apply small dabs of light color to the flowers, showing the forms in more detail. Work into the leaves behind with yellow and white, bringing out the shapes clearly.

Developing flower shapes

After the initial underpainting is completed in blues and greens, the artist blocks in flower shapes in a thin wash of red.

Working back into the flowers with a small bristle brush to heighten dark and light contrasts.

PAINTING OR drawing animals can be very different from working from the human figure. Because animals are rarely still, drawing or painting them is often an excellent exercise in learning how to work quickly to capture their essential characteristics. If, however, this proves impossible, photographs or pictures can be used as reference material instead of a live subject.

To translate the animal's movement into the painting, pick out characteristic curves and angles in the body and legs. Watch the animal carefully as it moves, looking for repeated movements. Utilize the texture of your brushstrokes to describe thick fur, feathers, or other textures and lay in small touches of color in the earth tones to enliven the overall image. Keep the background simple to focus attention on the color and patterns within the animal.

It can be interesting to use more than one animal in a painting, as the artist can then show more than one position, movement, or type of behaviour. Again, photographs, other pictures or rough sketches made 'on location' can be used as a base, with the various animals or positions of the same animal being combined into the final picture.

Materials

Surface
Prepared canvas board

Size
20in × 24in (50cm × 60cm)

Tools
Willow charcoal
Nos 5 and 7 flat bristle brushes
No 5 filbert bristle brush
Sheet of glass or palette
Tissue or rag

Colors

Black	Cadmium yellow
Burnt sienna	Gold ochre
Burnt umber	Ultramarine blue
Cadmium red	Yellow ochre

Medium
Turpentine

1. Draw up the outline shape in charcoal. Block in basic areas of tone with yellow ochre and blue-black.

2. Sketch in the pattern of stripes in blue-black, using a small bristle brush. Scrub in thin layers of color over the whole picture.

3. Work quickly over the shape of the animal with yellow, burnt sienna and white laying color into the black pattern. Angle the brush marks to accentuate form.

4. Adjust the proportions of the drawing and the division of the picture plane. Strengthen the blacks and heighten the colors, adding touches of red and blue.

5. Develop the tonal range in the background, spreading the paint with a rag. Work with black and brown to make a dense area of shadow.

6. Continue to work up the colors, dabbing in the shapes with a bristle brush, well loaded with paint to make a rich texture.

Blocking in background · lightening

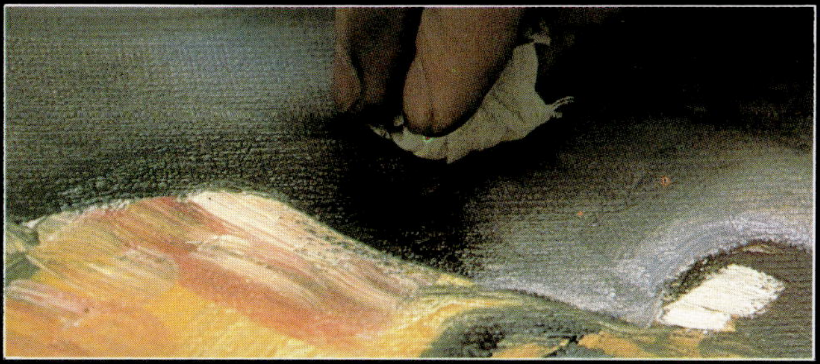

The artist rubs the background color into the surface with a tissue or piece of rag, to lighten the tone and pick up excess moisture.

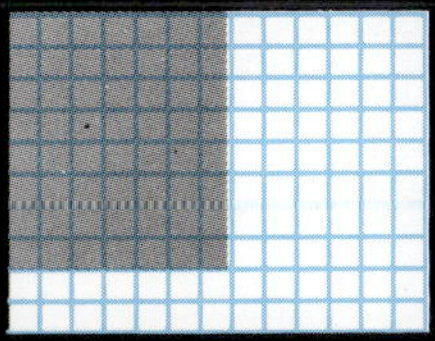

Using a thin wash of yellow ochre and black thinned with turpentine, the artist very loosely blocks in the background area, scrubbing the paint into the surface.

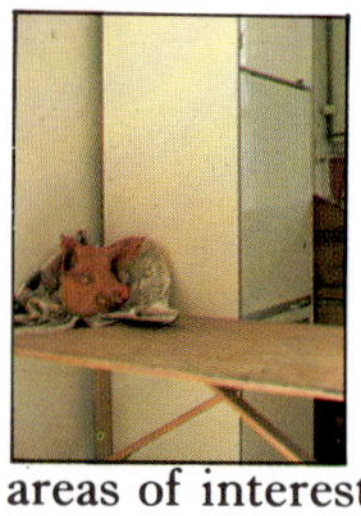

ONCE THE form and proportions of this painting were established in the initial drawing, the formal qualities of design, color, and texture became the major areas of interest. A study of the progress of this painting shows that the artist has made continual adjustments to the tones and colors, developing the image from a basic overall view rather than copying directly.

The paint surface is built up layer upon layer, with thin glazes first rubbed into the surface of the board. Thick impasto is applied with brushes and palette knives in craggy blocks of broken color or smooth opaque sweeps. Although the range of color is deliberately limited to exploit the tonal scale, the greys are varied across a wide range which contrast warm yellow hues and neutral or cool bluish tones. Areas of strong color, such as the pinks and reds of the pig's head, are established with the initial glazing then gradually covered and reglazed in the final stages.

The painting should be left to dry out at intervals as if the oil is laid on very thickly the paint will crack as it dries. The surface must be dry before the glazes are applied or the colors will merge and the clear sheen of the thin color will be lost.

Materials

Surface
Prepared canvas board

Size
24in × 20in (60cm × 50cm)

Tools
No 7 sable round brush
No 8 flat bristle brush
No 16 flat ox-ear brush
Assorted palette knives
Palette

Colors

Alizarin crimson	Ivory black
Burnt sienna	Payne's grey
Cadmium yellow	Prussian blue
Carmine	White
Cerulean blue	Prussian blue oil pastel

Mediums
Linseed oil
Turpentine

1. Draw the composition with Prussian blue oil pastel. Work over the drawing and block in tones with thinned Payne's grey with a No 16 brush.

2. Wash in layers of thin color – carmine and burnt sienna – over the table, the pig's head and the background, using the No 16 brush.

3. Mix cool, warm and neutral greys and spread thick paint over the background walls with palette knives and brushes. Work under the pig's head with white.

4. Work over the whole painting with impastoed layers of solid, textured color. Develop the form of the pig's head with pink, grey and white using a No 8 brush.

5. Continue to build up the layers of paint adjusting the tones of each shape until the whole surface is covered in cool and warm greys.

6. With a No 7 brush, draw into the pig's head with thick black lines and lighten the tone with palette knife and white paint. Rework the background tones.

7. Work over the forms with thin glazes of yellow-brown and dark grey, spread with rags.

8. Darken the tone of the whole work with thin layers of liquid glazes made from paint and linseed oil. Lay in bright pink and yellow tones over the pig's head.

Blocking in shapes · developing details

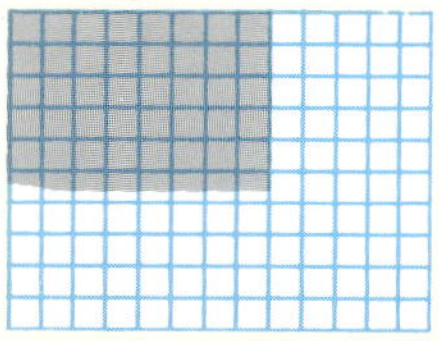

With a small bristle brush and ochre paint, the artist is here touching in the figure in the background.

Working with a large sable brush and thinned paint, the artist blocks in general color tones, rubbing the paint into the surface.

After the reddish underpainting has been allowed to dry, the artist begins to develop the pig's head in broad strokes of pale pinks and greys.

When the artist has modelled the head to satisfaction, a small sable brush and dark paint are used to put back in outlines and details.

Oil

IT IS INTERESTING to note in this painting that although the subject is a 'portrait' of peppers and a crab, the theme of the painting is predominantly non-objective. In fact, it is not so much the crab and peppers which determine the strength of the picture but their surroundings which, through the use of color, shape and texture, draws the viewer's attention into the center of the painting.

The environment is made up of flat shapes and planes described in neutral and earth tones which contrast with the roundness of the peppers and crab. Within the wall there are soft, blended tones and strokes which heighten the distinct lines and tones in the subject. The busyness of the checks in the cloth create a visual interest and, again, draw the viewer's eye into the center of the painting while the red cloth creates tension and contrast with the peppers and the stark white background. Note that the red used in the cloth is of a value purposely chosen to avoid overwhelming the rest of the picture with its 'redness' or contrasting too sharply with the green of the peppers.

Materials

Surface
Stretched, primed canvas

Size
35in × 30in (87.5cm × 75cm)

Tools
2B pencil
No 2 sable oil brush
Nos 4, 6 flat bristle brushes
Masking tape

Colors

Black	Cadmium yellow
Burnt sienna	Chrome green
Burnt umber	White
Cadmium red	Yellow ochre

Medium
Turpentine

1. With a 2B pencil, lightly put in the shapes and general composition of the painting.

2. Mix white and black and with a No 6 brush block in flat areas of color. With a a No 4 brush and more white, rough in outlines and shadows in the brick wall.

Details · describing cloth · masking tape

Masking tape is put down over the dried surface; when the shape has been blocked in, the tape is gently pulled away leaving a clean edge.

With a small sable brush, the artist works carefully into the shapes using smooth, consistent strokes.

Working over shadow areas in the checked cloth, the artist blocks in squares of pure black with a small sable brush.

6. With black and white, mix shades of grey. Using the No 2 sable brush, paint in squares of cloth using the white of canvas for white squares and light grey for shadow.

7. Work back into the checked cloth with a darker grey and black to strengthen light and dark contrasts.

3. With a No 2 brush and burnt sienna begin to develop the crab. In cadmium red, begin to define the red cloth.

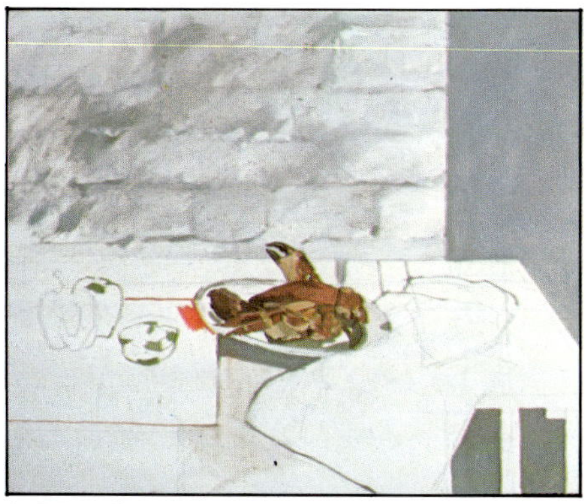

4. Mix chrome green and yellow and with the No 2 brush outline the peppers and put in light areas of color.

5. Mix umber, ochre, and white and block in the table with a No 6 brush. Add a touch of black to cadmium red and develop cloth shadows.

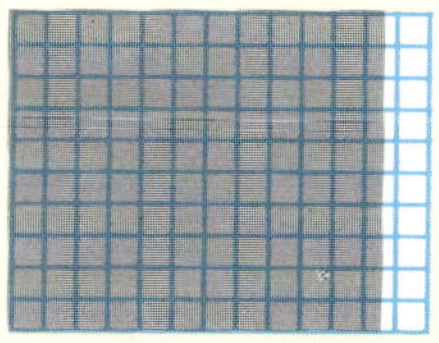

8. Mix white and ochre and lighten background bricks. Use the same grey tone as in the cloth to redefine brick outlines and shadows.

9. Mask the edge of the red cloth with tape and paint over this to create a clean, distinct edge.

10. With the No 2 sable brush and burnt umber, put in horizontal lines in the table and strengthen the shadow area in the table leg.

ACRYLICS WERE USED for the underpainting of this picture as they dry much faster than oils and allow the artist to begin to work in oils almost immediately. Note, however, that this process cannot be reversed and oils should not be used as an underpainting for acrylics.

The artist first tinted the canvas with a thin wash of acrylic paint because it is easier to see subtle color tones – especially white – when working on a non-white surface. A purple underpainting was used as a complement to the warm yellows and ochres which, when the underpainting shows through, creates the greenish tone of the finished work.

The color mixtures in this painting are both subtle and sophisticated. While this requires a good sense of color, all were created from the basic colors included in every artist's palette. Unity was achieved throughout the painting by adding small touches of a complementary color to the paint mixtures, such as adding yellow ochre to a predominantly purple tone or cerulean blue to a predominantly orange tone.

Materials

Surface
Stretched and primed canvas

Size
36in × 30in (90cm × 75cm)

Tools
Nos 4, 6 flat bristle brushes
No 2 round sable watercolor brush
Masking tape
Plates or palette
Newspaper or absorbent paper

Acrylic and oil colors

Black	Cobalt blue
Burnt umber	Cobalt purple
Cadmium red medium	Pthalo crimson
Cadmium yellow medium	White
Cerulean blue	Yellow ochre

Mediums
Turpentine
Poppy seed oil
Water

It is important to note that the artist altered the subject halfway through the painting process by exchanging the black boxes and neutral material for a yellow box and green fabric. This was done largely for compositional and interest reasons. The still life artist should feel free to rearrange or alter the subject to suit the painting or drawing.

1. Using acrylic paint, mix a wash of cobalt blue and burnt umber and block in the main outlines and shadow areas with a No 6 bristle brush.

3. Mix black and cobalt blue and put in dark shapes with a No 4 brush. Mix cerulean blue, yellow and white and block in the background.

5. To the above mixture add a small amount of white and cerulean blue. With a No 4 brush begin to describe the highlight areas of the face.

7. Add burnt umber to this mixture and lay in shadow on table. Lighten with white and put in highlight in cloth. Mix cerulean, yellow and put in background.

2. Use thinned pthalo crimson to block in the turban and background. Add cobalt purple for bluish areas. Mix cadmium red and yellow and block in the face and table.

4. With cerulean blue and white, put in light shape on left with a No 6 brush. Mix cadmium red, yellow ochre, and white and block in the light areas beside the head.

6. Mix white, cobalt blue and a small touch of black oil paint and block in the table shape. Add more black to make a darker tone; yellow ochre for warmer areas.

8. Carry the same background tone into the left foreground with a thinner wash of color.

(continued overleaf)

Underpainting · blocking in

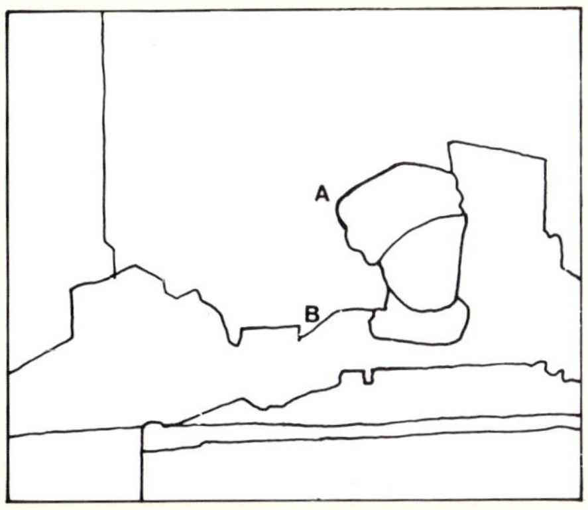

A. With a large brush and thinned acrylic paints, the artist blocks in general color areas scrubbing the paint well into the surface.

B. Once the acrylic underpainting has dried, broad areas of thick, opaque acrylic paint are blocked in.

9. Rework this entire area by painting over previous colors and shapes. Add black to greyish mixture and redefine box shapes with a No 4 brush.

10. Mix white, yellow ochre and a small amount of cerulean blue. With a No 2 sable brush, work in the face highlights with directional strokes.

11. With a thin mixture of permanent magenta and cobalt blue, darken the turban. Carry background color around cast to work around the head.

12. With the same brush and black paint, redraw the box shapes and outlines.

13. With cadmium yellow medium, put in box with a No 4 brush. Use masking tape to create a sharp, clean edge. Using the same yellow, blend into the table area.

14. Using the background tone with cerulean blue added, block in cloth shape to left. Mix white and cerulean blue and apply to the left hand area in even strokes.

15. Mix yellow ochre, burnt umber and white and put in highlights of books to right of case with a No 4 brush. Use same tone for box at left.

16. Add pthalo crimson to white mixture and put in warm tones of face and cloth with a No 2 sable brush.

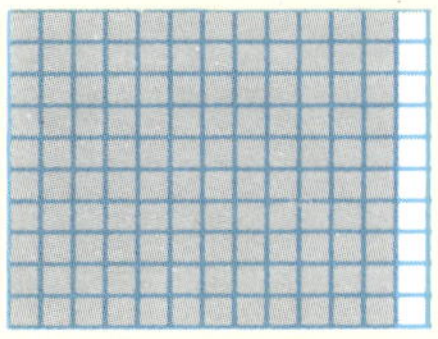

Masking tape · blotting · highlights

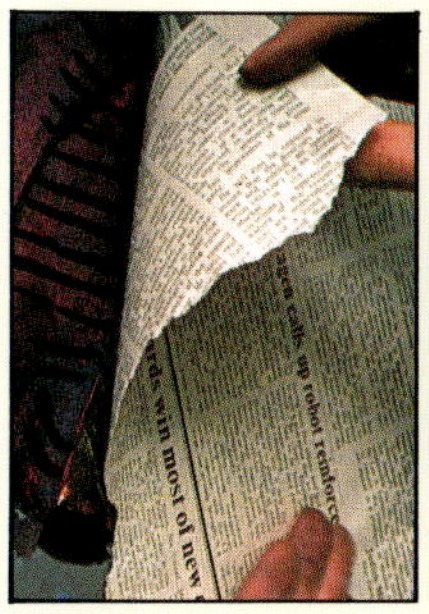

If the paint surface should become too wet to work on, a piece of newspaper can be laid over it, gently pressed with the hand, and slowly peeled off. This should not be attempted if the paint is very thick.

With a small sable brush the artist blocks in highlight and shadow areas in the cast. Note the use of the brushstroke to define structure.

Masking tape is a useful tool for creating clean, sharp lines and edges. Here the artist blocks in the box shapes over the tape. The tape is then carefully pulled off the surface.

A PREDOMINANTLY white painting will exercise all of the painter's skills. Preconceived ideas of the effects of color and light must be abandoned in favor of careful and thorough observation. This is thus an excellent way of training your eyes to see the many subtle tones and shades of color which exist in what is commonly believed to be a 'noncolor'.

One way of confronting the problem is to look at the subject in terms of warm and cool color areas. In this painting the white and grey tones are roughly divided between those created from the addition of blue – the cool tones – and those created by the addition of yellow – the warm tones. Until the middle steps of the painting, these warm and cool tones are exaggerated to allow the artist to correct or revise the tones as needed. In the last steps, the entire painting is gradually lightened to allow the subtle color variations to be revealed.

A wide range of marks are achieved by the confident handling of the bristle brushes. The artist has used both the tip and length of the brushes to vary the strokes and textures of the painting.

Materials

Surface
Prepared canvas board

Size
24in × 28in (70cm × 60cm)

Tools
Nos 3, 6 flat bristle brushes
Palette

Colors
Black
Chrome yellow
Cobalt blue
Raw umber
White

Medium
Turpentine

1. Mix a dark grey by adding a little blue to black and white. Thin the paint well with turpentine and sketch in the main areas of the composition with a No 6 brush.

2. Work over the drawing with the tip and flat of the brush, gradually increasing the detail. Aim for a loosely drawn impression of the whole subject.

3. Block in thin layers of paint to show the tonal changes across the image. Start to work over the drawing with thick patches of a lighter blue-grey.

4. With a range of warm and cool greys varied with blue and yellow mixtures, lay in shapes of solid color.

5. Extend the range of tones and build up the complexity of detail. Lighten the colors across the whole image with small dabs and strokes of thick paint.

6. Use the tip of the No 3 brush to draw into the shapes, emphasizing the linear structure and delicacy of the colors.

Outlining · underpainting

The thinned paint is rubbed into the surface – much like a charcoal drawing – to create a variety of tones. This underpainting will be used throughout the painting process to guide the artist in mixing the various shades and hues of white.

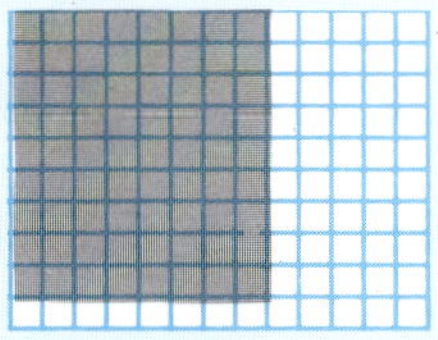

The artist is here using the tip of the brush and a very thin grey paint to draw in the basic shapes and composition of the picture.

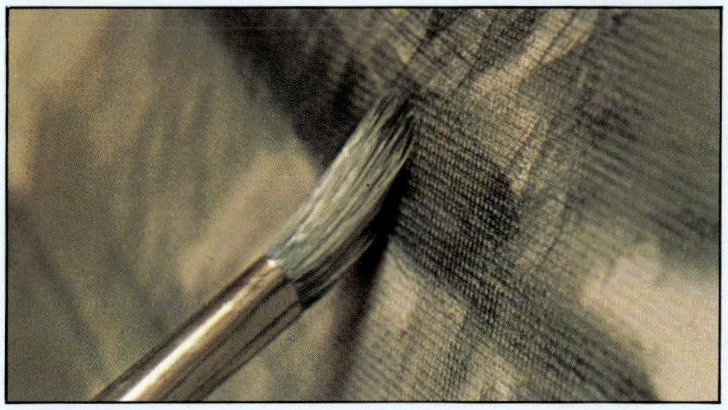

Oil

ONE OF the beauties of working in acrylics is that the artist can use them as a shortcut for the underpainting of oils without losing any of the brilliance of traditional oil underpainting. The artist can work quickly to block in general shapes and tones as a rough version to work from, or he can develop the underpainting to a nearly complete state and then finish off in oils. While at first glance this painting may seem to involve sophisticated color mixes and brushwork, most of the subtlety of tone and coloring is derived from the underpainting and the layering of thin washes of color one upon the other.

It is important to remember that the underpainting, whether executed in oil or acrylic, will have a strong effect on the finished picture. This is logical when you consider that the majority of drawings and paintings are done on white canvas to allow the pure, true brilliance of the color – regardless of media – to come through. No matter how thick, or opaque the paint mixture, the underpainting will affect the tones with subtle hints of color. The glass behind the figure is a good example of this, as nearly all the layers of color are in some way apparent in the finished picture.

Materials

Surface
Stretched and primed canvas

Size
27in × 30in (67cm × 75cm)

Tools
Nos 4, 6, and 10 flat bristle brushes
No 4 round sable brush
Palette

Colors

Acrylic:	*Oils:*
Cadmium red	Alizarin crimson
Cadmium yellow	Black
Hansa yellow	Cadmium red light
Mars black	Cadmium yellow
Pthalo green	Raw umber
Titanium white	Ultramarine blue
Ultramarine blue	White

Mediums
Water
Turpentine
Copal oil

1. With acrylic colors cadmium red, pthalo green and hansa yellow, apply the underpainting in a wet wash with a No 10 brush. Lay in general shadows.

2. Mix ultramarine blue and alizarin crimson and with a sable brush and ruler, put in the grid on the door.

6. Mix white and blue and with a No 6 brush work into the background area. With white and burnt umber, put in the woodwork and window.

7. With a No 4 brush mix oil colours cadmium red, yellow and a little blue for flesh tones. Mix black and blue and block in the hair. Use red for flowers.

Drawing the grid · blocking in hair · details

3. Mix hansa yellow and cadmium red in a wet wash and with the No 10 brush, cover door and flesh areas. Outline the figure with a small brush and burnt umber.

4. Put in the dark areas of the dress in a mixture of black and ultramarine blue. With an opaque orange, put in the reflections in the door and blend.

5. Mix a thin wash of orange and water and glaze over the face. With opaque white and a No 4 sable brush, block in the highlights in the face and blend lightly.

8. With a No 4 sable brush and pale blue, put in the hair highlights. Define the profile with burnt umber. Add touches of blue around the eyes for shadow areas.

9. Mix yellow ochre and white and put in warm highlight tones of the face. Blend a very light tone into the jawline. Add red and carry down the neck and chest.

10. Mix a pale tone from blue, white and umber and rub into the background. Heighten the reflection colors in the glass and blend. *(continued overleaf)*

After the underpainting has dried thoroughly, the grid on the door is drawn in using a ruler, fine pointed sable brush, and dark paint. Allowing the brush to drag across the rough canvas varies the tone of the line.

Working back into the cool underpainting of the face, the artist is here blocking in the hair and shadow areas with a thin wash of blue-black acrylic paint.

With a small brush and dark paint, the artist works over the dried underpainting indicating folds in the fabric and dress patterns.

Redefining grid · highlighting · refining profile

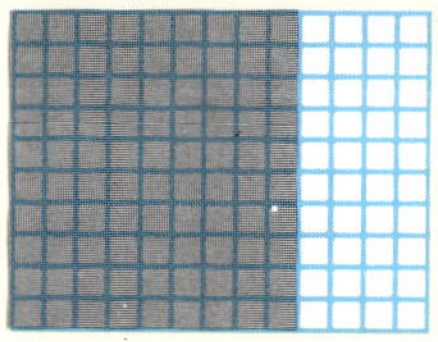

With a small sable brush and a light tone of grey, the artist puts in hair highlights using light quick strokes.

The original lines of the grid are redefined mid-way through the painting process.

Again using the small sable brush and opaque black paint, the profile of the sitter is cleaned up and further strengthened.

11. With the No 4 sable brush and a blue-black paint mixture, redefine the grid in the door with the ruler. Mix orange and water and glaze over the face.

12. Mix a light tone of white and cadmium red and work back into the face, strengthening highlights with a small brush.

13. With the same flesh tone, add a touch of green and lightly describe reflections in the mirror. Mix white, black, and blue and work over the light area behind the figure.

14. With orange and white, block in the arm. Work back into the reflections heightening light areas. Then, with black and blue, strengthen reflections

15. Put in the reflection of the hat with cadmium red. With white and yellow ochre, put in arm highlights

16. With a sable brush, put in details of hair and feather in hat. Strengthen highlight reflections in mirror with white and orange mixture.

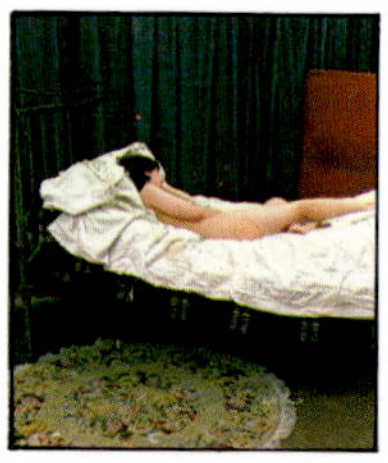

IN THIS painting the artist has let his imagination determine the techniques used. Rather than simply copying what was in front of him, elements of the subject have been used to create an interesting and atmospheric picture. While the artist used the subject largely for the preliminary stages of the painting, there was constant reference made to the model in the course of the work. Although the colors chosen are different from the actual subject, the artist used the general tones, highlights, and shadow areas within the model as reference and inspiration.

The painting was begun using the traditional technique of spreading a thin wash of color and turpentine over the surface to determine general tones and overall composition. It is interesting to note that the artist used brushes only for small areas of detail; the main body of the painting was executed with various shaped and sized palette knives. These allow a thick, opaque, juicy mixture of paint to be laid down and are especially useful for covering large areas. While it is difficult to render fine details with palette knives, the texture they create plus the broad planes of color can add a new dimension to an otherwise traditional technique.

Materials

Surface
Linen canvas, stretched and primed

Size
24in × 30in (60cm × 75cm)

Tools
Nos 4 and 8 flat bristle brushes
Assorted palette knives
Palette

Colors

Black	Gold ochre
Cadmium red medium	Lead white
Cerulean blue	Terre verte
Cobalt blue	Yellow ochre

Mediums
Turpentine
Linseed oil

1. With a No 8 brush, block in color areas with cerulean blue and light grey in a thin wash. Draw in the subject in pencil and blend colors with a small rag.

2. Use willow charcoal to reinforce outlines. Add more cerulean blue to color areas and blend. Put down charcoal and blend with turpentine and rag.

3. Mix cerulean blue and white and with a small palette knife lay in the figure and bed. Mix white, cerulean blue and black and describe the background and floor.

4. Add terre verte and block in the floor with a palette knife covering the surface. Work back into the walls, covering them thoroughly with the knife.

5. With pure white, brush in the figure and bed with a No 4 brush, covering the previous blue layer.

6. With a small palette knife, blend the rug out of the floor area. Lay in shadow areas with a darker floor tone and brush.

Finished picture · blocking in color · using palette knife · background area

The finished picture shows an interesting and innovative use of composition and technique. In particular this painting illustrates how a non-traditional approach to figure painting can yield interesting results.

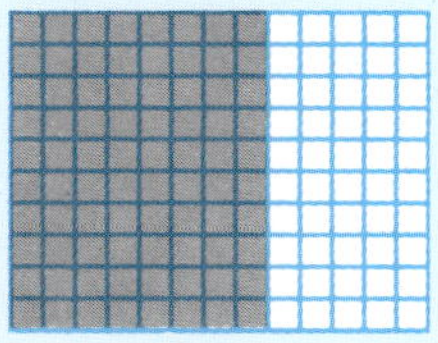

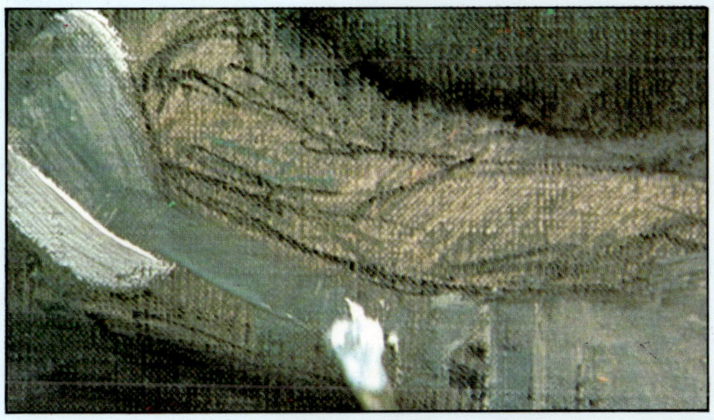

After the initial sketch has been described in charcoal, the artist begins to block in broad areas of color. The paint is allowed to bleed into the charcoal drawing. If this is not desirable, first dust the drawing lightly with a rag.

Using a Mahl stick and thin palette knife, the artist is here shown developing the background area.

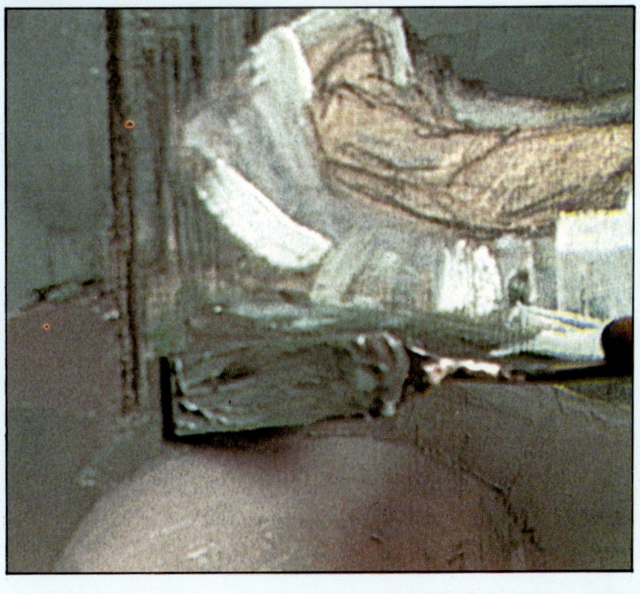

With a broad palette knife and a rich paint mixture, the artist puts in a layer of grey to describe the floor area.

FIGURE PAINTING is a highly individual process. There must be rapport between artist and sitter, or the painting will fail to capture the characteristics of both. It is important to remember that, while the artist is attempting to capture a superficial likeness, he is also trying to portray the essence, or personality, of the sitter as well. These aspects of portraiture should always determine the techniques used.

In this painting the artist has relied more on instinct than analysis and planning. This method requires self-confidence; it is not easy to boldly lay in free strokes without some anxiety over the outcome. With oil, however, if the artist lays down the wrong colour or shape, this can be easily scraped away and worked over.

The composition of this work is one of its outstanding features. The boldness of the colors and strokes and the oddly shaped chair arms serve to subtly emphasize the smallness of the figure without overpowering it and draw the eye inward.

By changing the background from white to taupe the artist has allowed the highlights and features of the child's face to come forward. The loose, white stroke at the bottom of the child's feet is repeated in the sleeves, and the odd shape emphasizes the natural liveliness of the subject.

Materials

Surface
Stretched and primed canvas

Size
18in × 20in (45cm × 50cm)

Tools
Nos 4 and 6 bristle brushes
No 2 sable brush
Palette

Colors

Burnt sienna	New blue
Cadmium green	Scarlet lake
Cadmium red deep	White
Chrome green	Yellow ochre

Mediums
Turpentine
Linseed oil

1. Mix burnt sienna and turpentine and with a small rag, rub into the surface. Dip a small No 2 sable brush in blue for outlines of figure and background.

2. With a No 4 bristle brush, block in the background with a thin wash of cadmium red. Thin blue and put in clothes. Use red and ochre for face.

3. Using cadmium green, block in chair seat with a No 6 brush. Put in arms of chair in red with a No 4 brush. Block in white background and blend.

4. Block in blue clothes in ultramarine. Use same white as for background to describe the arms. Rework the face with a mixture of ochre, white, and cadmium red.

5. With the same colour used for the face, put in the shadow of the chair. Mix white with cadmium red and put in chair highlights and blend with brush or rag.

6. With a very loose stroke, put in white pattern at bottom of figure. With another brush, put in sleeve details with ultramarine blue and define features.

7. Work back into the clothes with the skin tone, indicating highlights. Add touches of red to the face and details in a greenish tone with a small brush.

8. Mix burnt sienna, white, and red and cover the background. Use the same color in the face to strengthen shadow areas.

Finished picture · chair arms · facial details · blending with fingers

Besides employing a unique painting technique, the finished painting shows how much an interesting composition can add to any image. Especially in pictures of this type where the goal is to draw the viewer's eyes into the subject, attention should be paid to the placement of the figure.

Fingers are often useful tools for creating an interesting texture and stroke. After applying paint directly from the tube the artist here smooths out the color with a finger.

With a fine sable brush, the artist works back into the face to describe details. If the paint surface is still wet, these small lines of color can then be blended with a clean, dry brush.

Working over the dry underpainting, the artist blocks in the arms of the chair beside the child's right elbow.

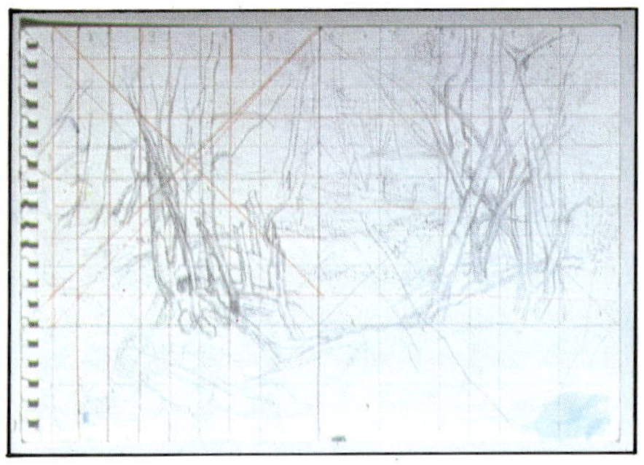

THE TECHNIQUE USED in this painting is a unique one which combines a number of extremely old painting methods. Fresco, tempera, and miniature painting techniques are all used, the results showing the inherent beauty of all of them. The basic technique is known as 'wet white'.

Because the artist must work in concentrated areas of detail – much like doing a needlepoint – this technique requires patience and a steady hand. It is a slow process and only very small areas can be covered at a time – thus its similarity to Renaissance fresco painting where only one area of a wall was worked on in the course of a day. The artist first mixes flake white and copal varnish, and applies a small amount to the surface. With a very fine sable brush and a touch of oil color thinned with turpentine, he then stipples a small area of color on to the white. The white/varnish mixture has the effect of bringing forth a jewel-like quality in the paint, which lends translucence and depth to the overall effect.

Until the paint dries, the area worked on is flexible and movable. It can be altered, corrected or worked on until the paint dries – approximately a day. If the artist is dissatisfied with the results, he can overpaint, but this must be done while the paint is wet.

Materials

Surface
Primed hardboard

Size
12in (30cm) diameter

Tools
Nos 2 and 4 sable brushes
Palette or plate

Colors
Alizarin crimson
Cadmium green
Cadmium red
Cadmium yellow
Cerulean blue
Cobalt blue
Flake white

Mediums
Copal oil varnish
Turpentine

Finished picture
overpainting with white · pure color strokes · brushstrokes

The special technique used to create this picture is best understood through the use of close-up shots of the work. For this reason, the picture has not been presented in steps.

A thin layer of flake white and copal varnish are laid down over the transferred drawing. While still wet, using a fine sable brush and ultramarine blue, the artist stipples in dots of paint, following the pencil outline.

Rather than mixing colors separately on a palette, this technique involves creating colors and tones directly on the surface by overlaying thin strokes of pure color.

This detail shows the particular brushstrokes required when using the 'wet white' technique. Note in particular the small touches of complementary color applied with small, light touches over the green underpainting to create depth.

PRECISION AND METHOD are the keywords for the technique used in this painting. Each area is painted in some detail so that the whole image gradually emerges piece by piece. At each new stage, the previous work is adjusted to ensure that the color and tonal relationships of the whole image are balanced

The range of color is limited and the palette consists primarily of earth colors. Cool grey shadows contrast with warm tones within the figure and these warm tones are enlivened by touches of vermilion. The dark greys in the chair and background wall are mixed from black and white, with the addition of ultramarine.

Use masking tape to establish clean outlines. Lay broad strips along the straight lines and define curves with narrow tape which can be manipulated into irregular shapes. Rub down the edges of the tape firmly before you paint over it and lay in areas of flat colour with large bristle brushes. Pull off the tape slowly and carefully to leave a clean, sharp edge.

Materials

Surface
Stretched and primed cotton duck

Size
39in × 30in (98 cm × 76cm)

Tools
HB Pencil
No 8 round sable brush
Nos 3, 7 flat bristle brush
Palette
1in (2.5cm), ¼in (.62cm) masking tape

Colors

Black	Vermilion
Burnt sienna	White
Burnt umber	Yellow ochre
Raw umber	

Medium
Turpentine

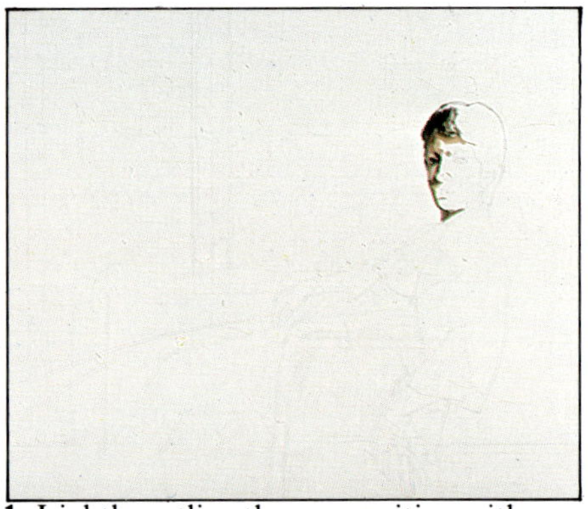

1. Lightly outline the composition with an HB pencil. With a No 8 sable brush, work into the face and hair with black and mixtures of sienna, vermilion, and white.

2. With a No 7 brush, block in flesh tones over the forehead and black and burnt umber in the hair. Work on details around eyes and nose with light browns.

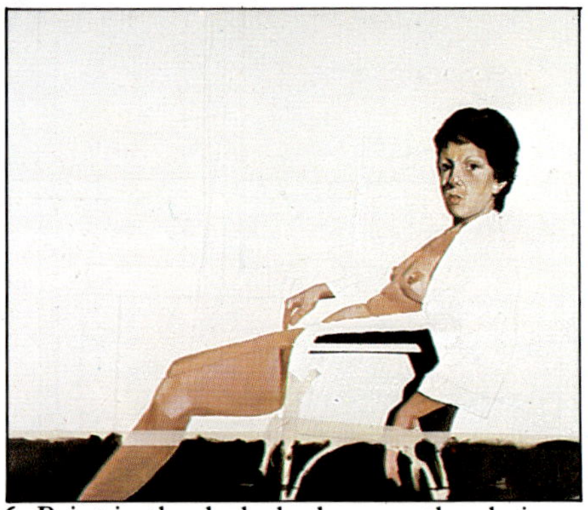

6. Paint in the dark shadows on the chair with a mixture of burnt umber and black. Mask off the lines of the floor and chair legs with tape and block in dark brown.

7. Develop the background using masking tape to make straight lines. Fill in the shapes with yellow ochre and a dark red-brown directly behind the figure.

Masking tape · background · face and chair details

Masking tape can be useful for creating sharp, clean edges (below). When working with irregular shapes, use a narrow tape which can be manipulated into curves.

With a small brush, the artist blocks in the background area around the figure.

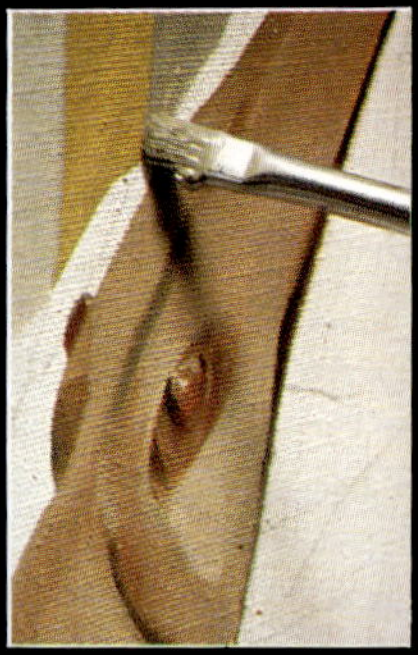

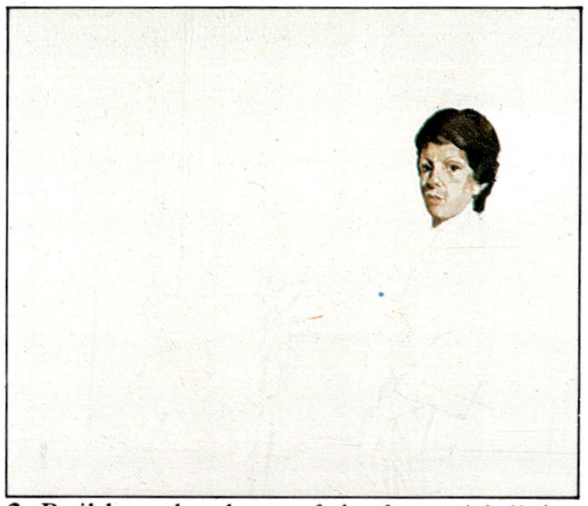

3. Build up the shape of the face with light pink tones and brown shadows, blending the colors together. Emphasize the mouth and nose with vermilion and white.

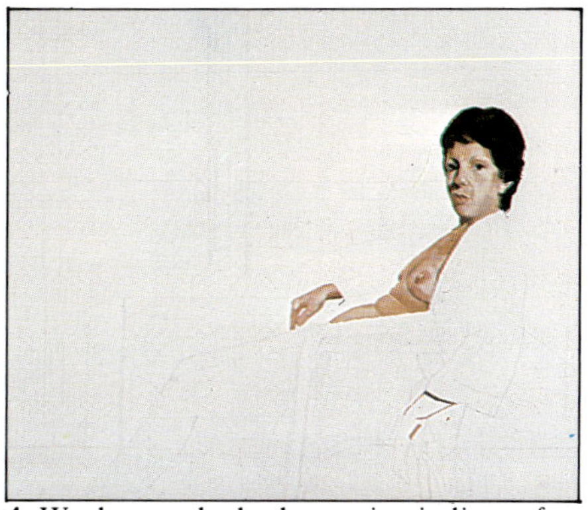

4. Work over the body putting in lines of shadow with burnt umber and blending flesh tones into the shapes. Draw up the hands and block in solid color.

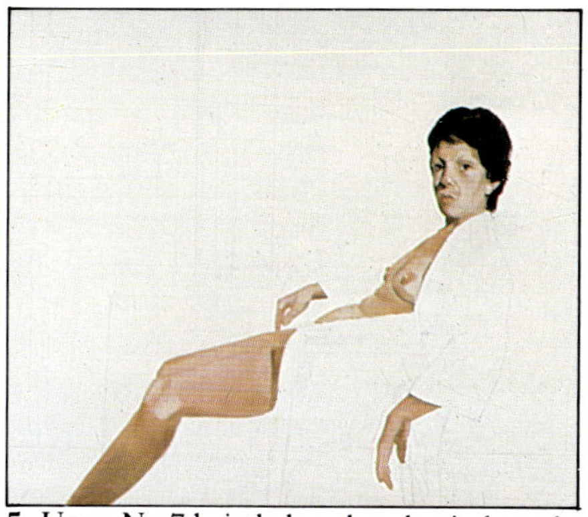

5. Use a No 7 bristle brush to lay in broad areas of tone in the legs. Adjust colors over the entire figure and add strong white highlights.

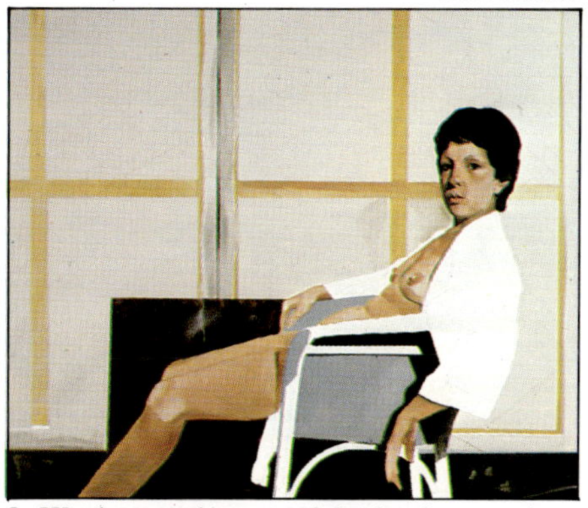

8. Work over the rest of the background with a warm, pale beige, thinly shadowed with grey. Paint a thick layer of light grey over the chair and wall to right.

9. Work back over the head of the figure with a No 3 brush. Lay in a thin grey shape behind the model to depict shadow.

10. Brush in folds and creases on the jacket in black and blend with thick white paint to make mid-toned greys. Build up the woven pattern of the chair in white.

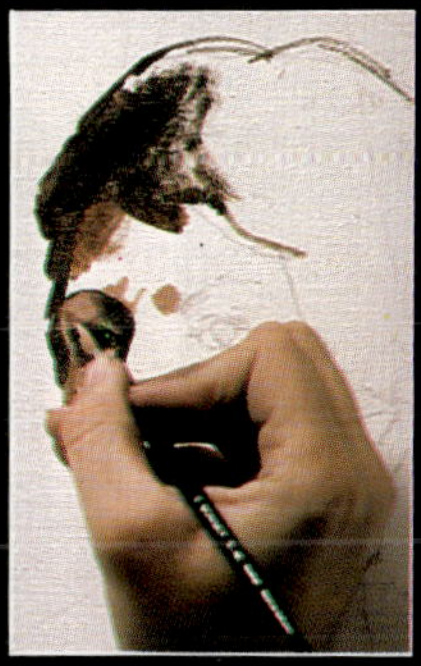

With a fine sable brush, the artist begins to develop small areas of detail around the eyes.

Once the surface is thoroughly dry, the artist returns to put in the fine weave of the chair with a small pointed sable brush and pure white paint.

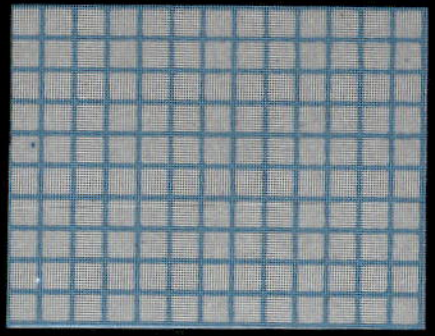

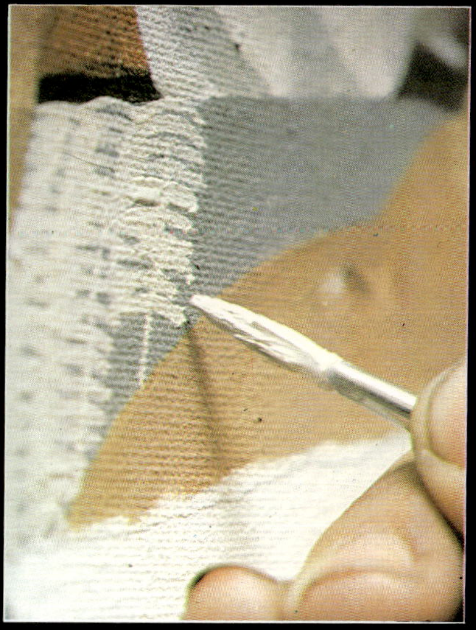

WHILE MOST of the activity in this painting centers around the figure and the chair as the central objects, the surrounding area also plays a crucial part in the success of the work as a whole.

By following through the steps, the method used by the artist becomes clear. Whether working on shadow areas or highlights, figure or background, blending and softening or defining and accentuating, the painting evolves through the constant and deliberate interplay of colors between figure and background. In looking carefully at the finished painting, you will see that all the colors used in the background are also contained in the figure. The broad planes of color describing floor and walls all move toward the figure, where they are concentrated, emphasized and modulated. The artist worked over the entire surface simultaneously; the figure was never altered without changing the environment, and vice versa.

The geometric shapes of the background – the strong verticals, horizontals and diagonals – emphasize the softness of the figure as a soft, malleable feature in a world of planes and edges. The warm tones in the figure and chair serve to separate it from its environment, which is predominantly cool and impersonal.

Materials

Surface
Prepared canvas board

Size
18in × 24in (45cm × 60cm)

Tools
No 10 round sable brush
No 4 flat bristle brush
Palette

Colors

Alizarin crimson	Chrome oxide
Burnt sienna	Raw sienna
Burnt umber	Ultramarine blue
Cadmium red	Yellow ochre

Mediums
Linseed oil
Turpentine

1. Mix burnt sienna and white. With a No 10 sable brush, block in the figure. With burnt umber, block in the ground area.

2. Add white to the burnt umber and start to block in the area surrounding the figure. Using the same mixture, begin to develop shadow areas within the figure.

4. Dip a No 4 brush in linseed oil and blend the previous color areas within the figure. Cover the remaining background area in green mixture.

5. Apply cadmium red directly from tube on to chair. Mix green and ochre and blend with rag or finger. Use a lighter tone of same in the background.

7. Mix alizarin crimson, blue and white and rework shadow areas in figure and background. Carry this into the foreground with a flicking motion.

8. Mix chrome green, white, and a touch of red and block in shape on the right. Carry this into the background. Lighten with white and use for highlights.

3. Mix chrome green and white and put in background. Apply cadmium red medium for the chair: white and ochre for highlights, and burnt umber for hair.

6. Mix red and white and put in the chair highlights. Carry this into the figure for highlight areas. Use pure burnt sienna to describe shape at left.

9. Develop final details of painting with white and yellow ochre. Mix white and umber for face features. With chrome green and yellow put in strip on left.

Blotting with tissue

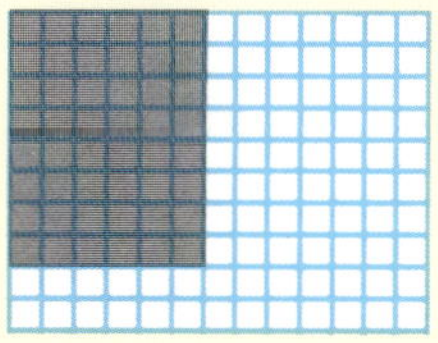

If the paint surface becomes too wet, excess moisture can be blotted up with a small piece of tissue. Do not rub into the surface but simply press the tissue down lightly.

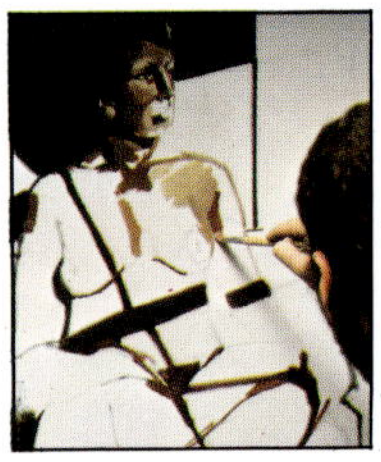

IN ORDER to bring out the full tonal qualities of the subject, here the artist has used a narrow range of colors, relying on strong light and dark contrasts to disrupt what would otherwise be a predictable harmony. The result is a powerful image in which the figure is clearly recognizable, but with an element of abstraction in the pattern of the shadow and the broad planes of color.

The pattern of shapes in a painting is a crucial factor, so you should map out the composition carefully at the start. Follow the outlines as you apply the paint but keep the brushwork loose and vigorous. Thin the paint with turpentine and use long-handled bristle brushes in fluid strokes, gradually tightening up the image as the painting develops.

Color must be used carefully to differentiate the dark tones as otherwise the shapes will merge together. Enrich the heavy shadows by adding blue or brown to black paint. Adjust light tones continuously until you are satisfied with the result. Note that here the light yellow has been made more vivid in the final stage and extended over the orange shape to cool the contrast. None of the highlights are made from pure white and the intensity of the image is maintained through the relationship of the colors and the tones rather than through light and dark areas.

Materials

Surface
Stretched and primed cotton duck

Size
36in × 30in (90cm × 76cm)

Tools
No 6 flat bristle brushes
No 6 round sable brush
1in (2.5cm) decorators' brush
Palette

Colors

Black	Raw umber
Burnt sienna	Ultramarine blue
Burnt umber	Vermilion
Cadmium yellow	Yellow ochre

Medium
Turpentine

1. Sketch in the outlines with an HB pencil and then draw with a No 6 sable and black paint, using line and small areas of tone to establish the basic structure.

2. Draw up the central shadow across the figure with burnt sienna. Work into the flesh tones on the face and lay in the dark shadow behind the head.

3. Develop the linear pattern, plotting the contour of the figure and shadows. Work into the face in more detail and block in a solid background tone.

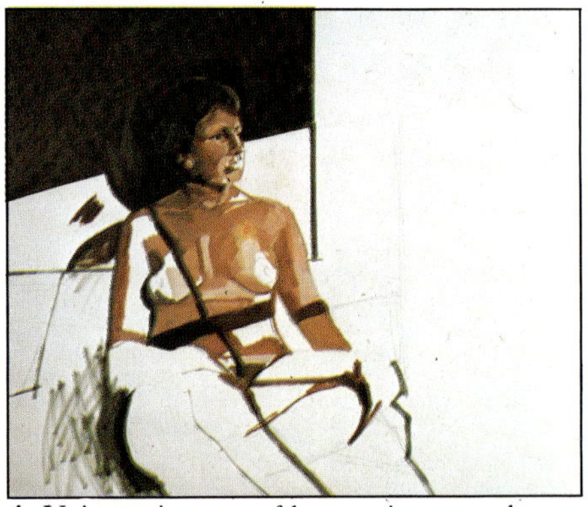

4. Using mixtures of burnt sienna and white with red and yellow, develop tones within the figure.

5. Continue to work in flat patches of flesh tones, brushing the colors together. Lay in reddish-brown behind the figure and dark blue shadows with a No 6 bristle.

6. Mix yellow ochre with raw umber and use a No 6 brush to block in the right-hand side of the background. Cover the white space, scrubbing into the canvas.

7. Work over the lower half of the figure with loose brushstrokes in dark brown tones. Contrast the shadows with a light yellow tone showing the fall of light.

8. Enrich the foreground colour with a solid shape of bright orange and warm tones in the legs, covering the remaining canvas. *(continued overleaf)*

Shadow areas · eye highlights · flesh tones

The shadow area beside the head is created with a dark tone thinned with turpentine. This is later covered over with a thicker layer of paint. The painting should develop through many thin layers of overpainting rather than a few thick layers.

With a fine sable brush, the artist puts in highlight areas around the eye.

A mid-toned flesh color is blended into a shadow and highlight area. The paint is first laid down and then blended by using a clean, dry brush.

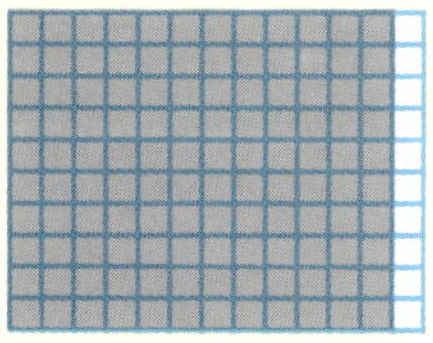

Figure shadows and blending

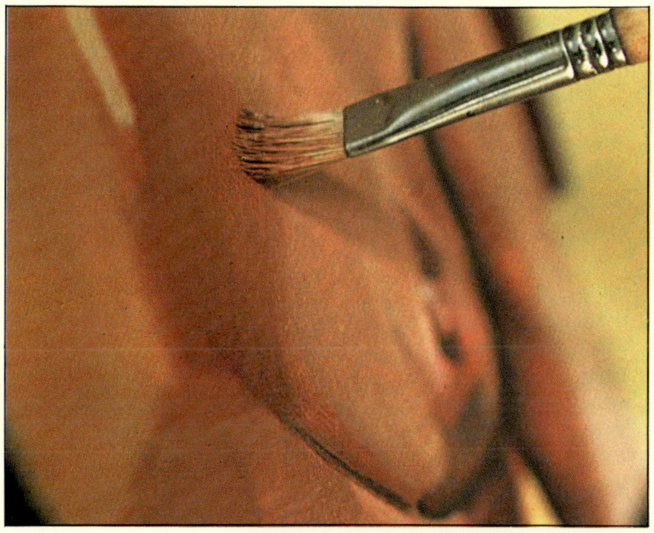

Shadow areas in the torso are described with a medium-sized sable brush. This color area is next blended into surrounding colors.

9. Revise the skin tones in the upper part of the figure, smoothly blending the color.

10. Continue to work over the whole image making adjustments in the color values. Lay in a dark blue-black shadow down the right leg of the figure.

11. Lighten the tones across the central section of the painting and even out patches of loosely worked color, blending them into smooth, fluid shapes.

12. Break down the foreground shapes to show the pattern of cast shadow over the legs. Strengthen dark tones with black and dark blue.

Oil

IN ART HISTORICAL terms, the technique of working on a stark, white canvas is a recent development made popular by the Impressionists of the last century. Before that time it was customary to work on a colored ground, made either by mixing pigment into the priming coat or laying a thin wash of color over a white base. The purpose of this was to establish a middle tone over which to work with light and dark colors and to give the image a warm or cool cast.

The red priming used in this painting is a powerful color which radically affects the whole character of the painting. The forms are constructed with a variety of greys; those which tend toward blue or green are emphasized on the strong red ground, and pink and yellow flesh tones pick up the warm glow of red which breaks through. Although the palette is limited, the relationships of the colors are vibrant and active. You will need to pay close attention to both the subject and the painting to achieve a lively but controlled result.

Use thick, dry paint and keep the brushwork loose and open so the red is seen through the broken color. Stiff bristle brushes are effective for this if handled lightly and vigorously. Keep the paint dry, adding only a small amount of turpentine, or the colors will flood the surface and deaden as they dry out.

Materials

Surface
Canvas primed with red oil-based primer

Size
30in × 26in (75cm × 65cm)

Tools
Nos 3, 6, flat bristle brushes
Palette

Colors

Black	Foundation white
Chrome yellow	Oxide of chromium
Cobalt blue	Permanent rose

Medium
Turpentine

1. Use a No 6 bristle brush to block in the basic shape of the figure in white. With a No 3 brush, sketch in the outline and lay areas of light tone.

2. Mix two tones of grey from cobalt blue, black and white. Work over the whole canvas in thin patches of color.

3. Develop the dark tones around the hat, shoulders and neck. Add a little yellow to the greys and block in the tones behind the head and in the hat.

4. Work into the face and neck with a light greenish-grey, roughly mapping out the features. Build up the structure of the image, with detail in the hat and collar.

5. Develop the color in the face using cool blue-grey contrasted with a warm flesh tone mixed from yellow, rose, and white. Indicate features with light marks.

6. Draw into the features with dark red, black and white. Block in light tones on the shirt with solid grey and white.

7. Work over the whole image with thick paint developing the tonal structure with warm greys in the foreground and light grey-green in the background.

8. Work over the figure with a No 3 brush, dabbing in color to refine details and add definition to the features.

Finished picture · outlining in white · scratching back

By completion of the painting, (above) the strong red underpainting is almost completely obscured, yet its subtle influence can be seen in the warm cast of the image.

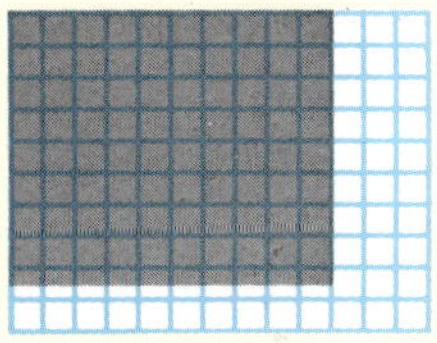

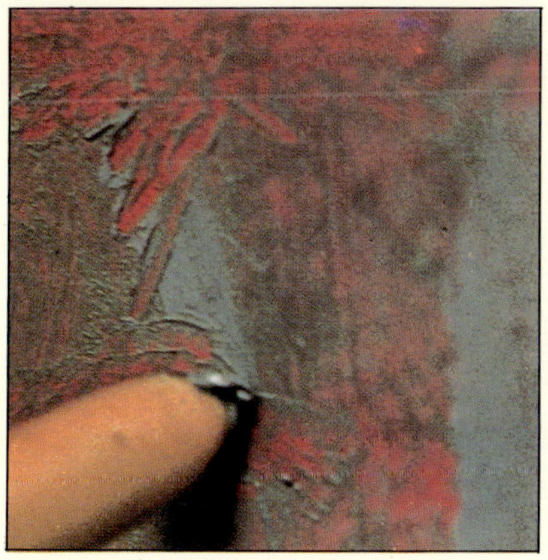

Using the end of the brush, the artist is here scratching back through the wet paint layer to allow the underpainting to break through to the surface.

Using undiluted white paint, the artist roughs in the general composition and figure outlines over the dry red underpainting.

ONE OF THE most interesting aspects of this painting is how few colors were used to effectively render the subject and its environment. The artist has relied only upon tones of burnt umber, burnt sienna, ochre, and white for almost the entire painting. This stresses the wisdom of the artist familiarizing himself with the many color mixes that can be attained from using a limited palette. The knowledge gained from working in this way is greater than using a variety of colors as the same principles apply to using many colors as to using a few. Thus the knowledge and experienced gained by using a limited palette can later be used with any number of colors.

The strength of the picture comes not only from the simplicity of the palette, but from the composition as well. This is – as any successful composition should be – not obvious, but has the subtle effect of directing the viewer's attention where the artist intends it to go. The artist intentionally left a great deal of space around the figure. Coupled with the pale strip down the right hand side and the off-centre placement of the subject, the viewer's eyes are drawn directly into the figure.

Materials

Surface
Primed cotton duck

Size
23in × 30in (57cm × 75cm)

Tools
HB pencil
Nos 2 and 4 flat bristle brushes
No 5 sable round watercolor brush
1½in (3.75cm) housepainting brush
Fixative
Palette

Colors

Black	Raw sienna
Burnt sienna	Scarlet lake
Burnt umber	White
Cobalt blue	Yellow ochre

Medium
Turpentine

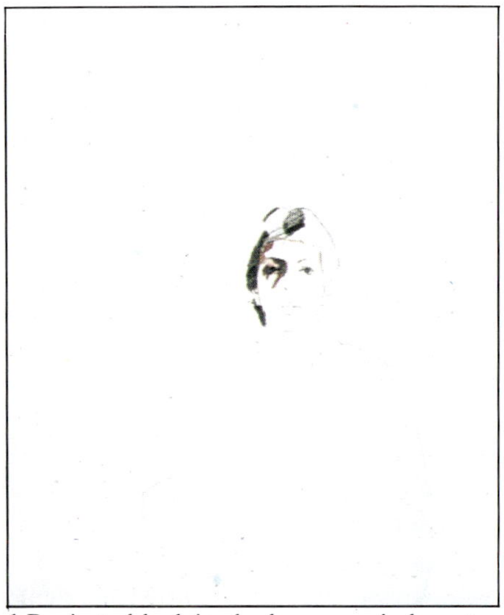

1 Begin to block in shadow areas in burnt and raw sienna with a No 5 sable brush. Add white to the sienna and work into the eye area in detail with a No 2 brush.

2 Continue to block in the shadows of the face with a thinned mixture of burnt umber and white.

3. Continue to block in highlight areas with white and ochre. Add a touch of scarlet lake to warm the flesh tones.

4. Put in mouth details with the No 2 brush and scarlet lake, yellow ochre and white. Add touches of highlight in the ear. Blend again with a clean, large brush.

5. Begin to lay in the pattern of the jacket with loose strokes of burnt umber with a No 4 brush. Rough in the outline of the arm and scrub in the shadow area.

6. Next block in lighter jacket areas in yellow ochre. With a 1½in (3.75cm) housepainting brush, blend tones together.

(continued overleaf)

Initial drawing · modelling face · blending highlights

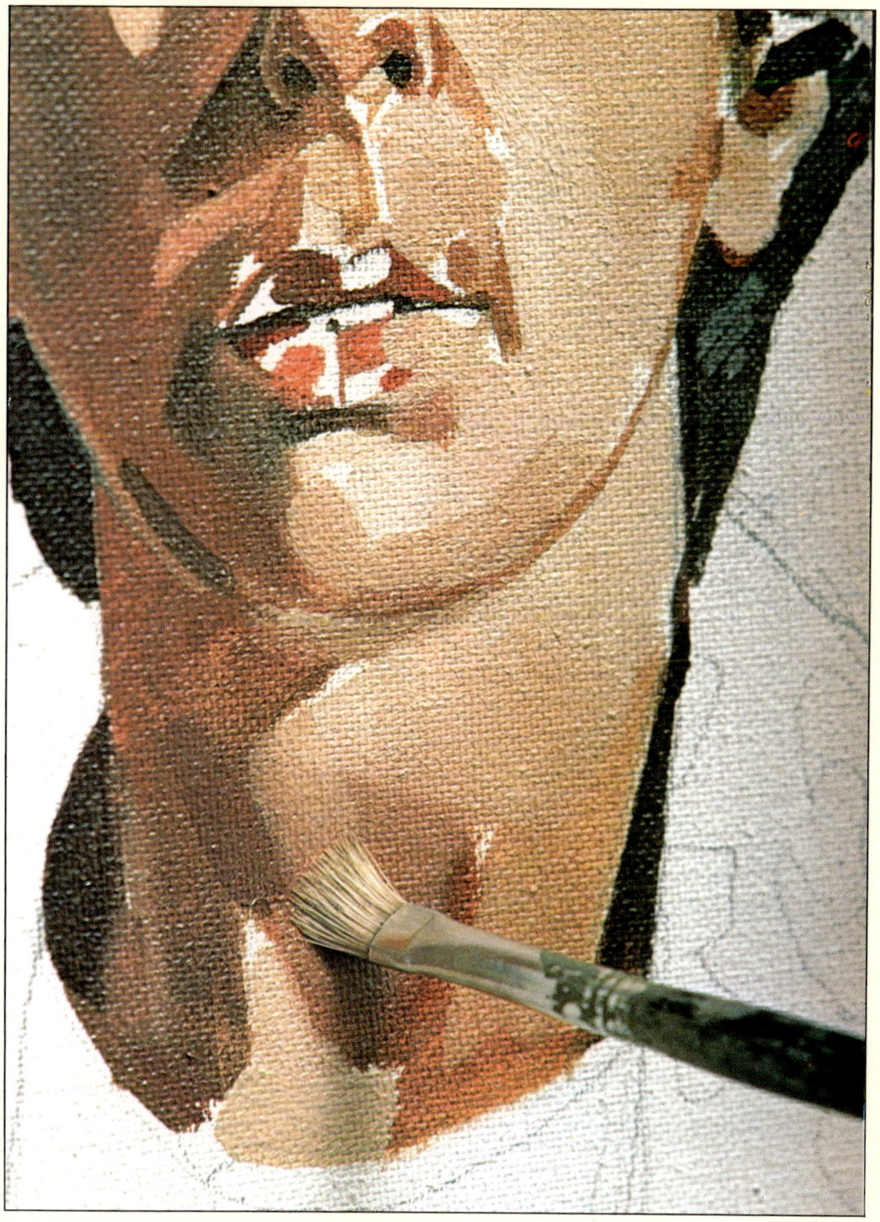

The figure is first drawn in with light pencil strokes (top) including as much detail as possible. Using a small sable brush and warm and cool flesh tones, the artist begins to model the face of the figure (above) working from one point outwards. Moving downwards, larger areas of highlights are blocked in and then blended into surrounding areas with a dry, clean brush (right).

Coat pattern · working inside and outside the figure

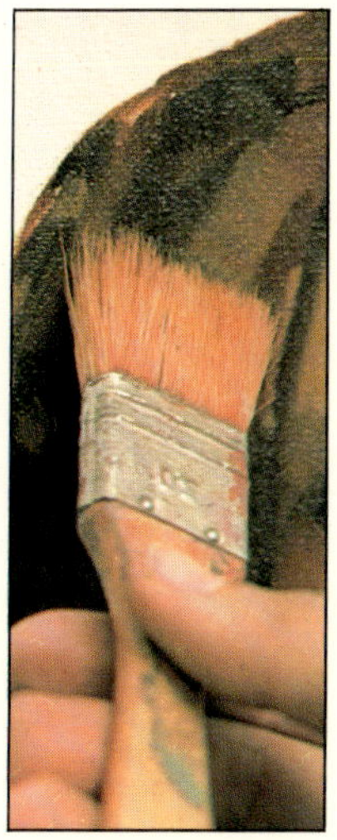

To create the pattern of the coat, the artist first describes the lighter pattern and fills in the white areas with a darker tone. Then, with a clean, dry decorators' brush, the colors are blended together with a feathering motion, the brush just lightly touching the surface.

Working outside the figure(above), the background is roughed in with the decorators' brush. A clean edge between background and figure is obtained by using a smaller brush and background color. Moving into the figure (left), the shirt is carefully described in tones of grey and white.

7. Continue to define the pattern in burnt umber and fill in with yellow ochre. Darken shadow area around collar. Block in the right side with burnt sienna.

8. Continue to put in the pattern in burnt umber and yellow ochre. Mix scarlet lake and yellow ochre for the highlight areas. Rough in the shirt shadow in grey.

9. With a No 4 brush and grey paint, block in the shirt. With burnt sienna, raw umber, and the housepainting brush, cover the background area.

10. Smooth out the background with the housepainting brush and a lighter brown made from burnt umber and white.

11 Work back into the right side of the jacket with gold ochre, scrubbing in highlight areas.

12. Block in the pattern with the no 4 brush and burnt umber.

THE PORTRAIT shown was executed quickly. However, because a very rich mixture of paint and oil medium was used, the painting had to be allowed to dry thoroughly between stages to avoid muddying the colors and surface.

The artist was chiefly concerned with the fine details of the painting – for example the model's features – until the final steps. In these last few steps broad, general areas of the figure were tightened up and the final detailed touches – those which turned the work from a figure painting into a portrait – were put into the painting.

The subject was never treated as a series of parts – face, torso, legs and arms – but was always considered as a complete unit throughout the painting process. Thus, if the artist applied a highlight in the face, he might very well use this same color in the dress and hands. This method of painting unifies the image by the use of similar colors placed throughout the figure. As well, it prevents the artist from seeing the subject as a number of parts, but as a whole unit in which every area – no matter how small – directly affects every other area.

Materials

Surface
Prepared canvas board

Size
14in × 18in (35cm × 45cm)

Tools
No 6 flat bristle brush
No 4 sable round brush
Palette

Colors

Alizarin crimson	Cobalt blue
Black	Terre verte
Burnt umber	White
Cadmium red light	Yellow ochre

Mediums
Turpentine
Linseed oil

Blending with fingers · describing hands

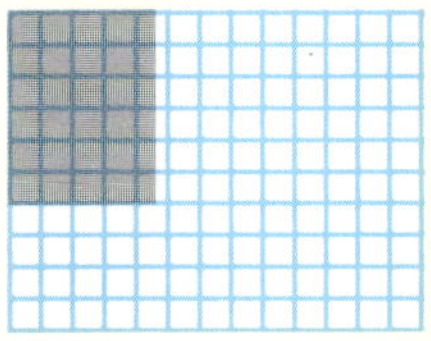

The artist has purposely avoided using small areas of detail except in the face of the model. Details are not always needed to accurately and effectively render a subject, as seen in the sitter's hands.

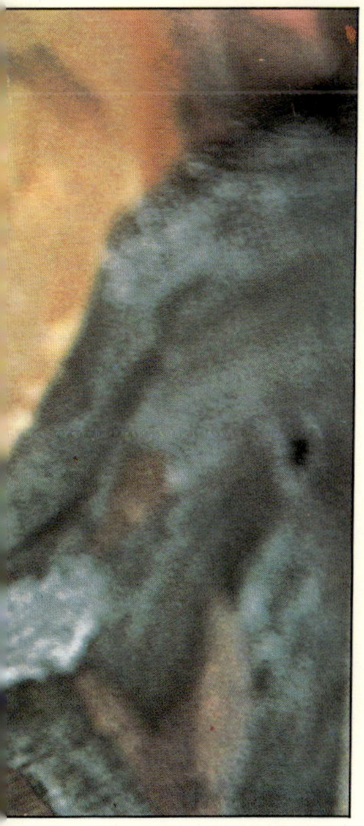

Rather than using a brush or rag, the artist is here using his fingers to blend the figure's shoulder into the background. Blending with the fingers produces a subtle, smudged effect unobtainable by other means.

1. With red, yellow ochre, and a mixture of blue and alizarin crimson, block in the general color areas of the figure in a thinnish wash with a No 6 brush.

2. Add white to these colors and block in the lighter areas of the figure with long strokes. Using the color of the skirt highlight, put in the strip on the left side.

3. Block in the hair with burnt umber and a No 4 sable brush. Mix terre verte, white, and linseed oil and loosely put in general facial features. Blend left side of coat.

4. Using cobalt blue and black, work into the dark shadow areas of the skirt. With the same tone, loosely block in shadows on the left side of the shirt.

5. Mix white, terre verte, and a small amount of cobalt blue and block in grey area to left. Work into the left side of the face with terre verte and white.

6. Put in scarf details in blue and white. mix grey tone and put in brick details behind figure. Touch in dark details of face and skirt highlights.

WHILE A SUCCESSFUL portrait is never an easy thing to achieve, there are certain techniques which will facilitate the process.

In terms of capturing a likeness, the key to a successful portrait is to make sure that the first basic step – the preliminary drawing – is as accurate as possible. If the features are not correctly positioned and described at the outset, there is little chance of success and the artist will find himself repeatedly laying down paint, scraping it off, and reworking in an attempt to correct the original drawing.

Once the preliminary work is as accurate as possible, do not be over-concerned with details. The most important thing at this stage is to check and recheck the positioning of the features while you work. A face is not made up of a series of individual parts; always judge distance and relative size by comparing one feature to another.

If you work in thin rather than thick washes of color, there is less danger of building up the paint surface too quickly. It is easier to correct and revise thin layers of paint then thick. Work in light-dark and warm-cool tones and keep the palette as simple as possible. The artist here used a minimum of colors, with the addition of white, to successfully capture the subject of the portrait.

Materials

Surface
Prepared canvas board

Size
9in × 10in (22.5cm × 25cm)

Tools
No 6 flat bristle brush
No 4 round sable brush
Palette

Colors
Burnt sienna
Burnt umber
Cadmium red deep
Gold ochre
White

Mediums
Turpentine
Linseed oil

1. With a No 4 sable brush and a wash of turpentine and burnt umber, block in outlines, facial features and the start of the background.

2. With a No 6 bristle brush, block in the hair in gold ochre and background in thinned umber. Use burnt sienna and white for the face tones.

3. Mix a deeper shade of burnt umber and paint over background. Work into the hair. With burnt sienna and white put in shadow areas on right.

4. Put in lips with cadmium red and white mixture. Put in touches of dark shadow with the sable brush and burnt umber.

5. With pure cadmium red, paint in the necklace. Mix warmish tones of burnt sienna, red and white and work over the face. blending in the paint.

6. With a mixture of burnt umber and white, re-define the facial planes with even strokes. Mix white, cadmium green and yellow ochre and cover in the background.

Hair shadows

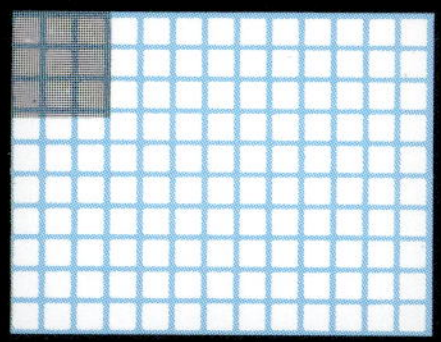

Shadow areas in the hair are put in with fluid brushstrokes and a neutral, mid-toned grey.

THE TECHNIQUES USED for this portrait demonstrate an oil painting method which is essentially direct and spontaneous both in the drawing and application of color. As the painting was completed in only two sittings, the paint had no time to dry. For this reason the artist would occasionally blot the painting surface with a rag or sheet of paper to lift excess moisture.

A color photograph rather than live subject was used for the painting, but the information supplied was used only for the groundwork of the painting and the end result is not a straightforward copy. Photographs tend to flatten subtleties of tone and color, so it is necessary to add to the image by strengthening or even exaggerating certain elements. In this example, the background color and patterns in the clothes were altered as the painting progressed.

Work rapidly with stiff bristle brushes to block in the overall impression of the image, using the brushmarks to indicate the structure and texture of the forms. Small sable brushes are more suitable for adding fine points of detail. Experiment with colour mixes on a separate piece of paper or board to find the right tones for subtle flesh colours and shadows.

Materials

Surface
Primed hardboard

Size
12in × 18in (30cm × 45cm)

Tools
No 3 flat bristle brush
No 5 sable round brush
Newspaper
Palette

Colors

Alizarin crimson	Ultramarine blue
Black	Vermilion
Cadmium yellow	Van Dyke brown
Chrome oxide	White
Cobalt blue	Yellow ochre

Mediums
Turpentine
Linseed oil

Face shadows · eye details · blotting

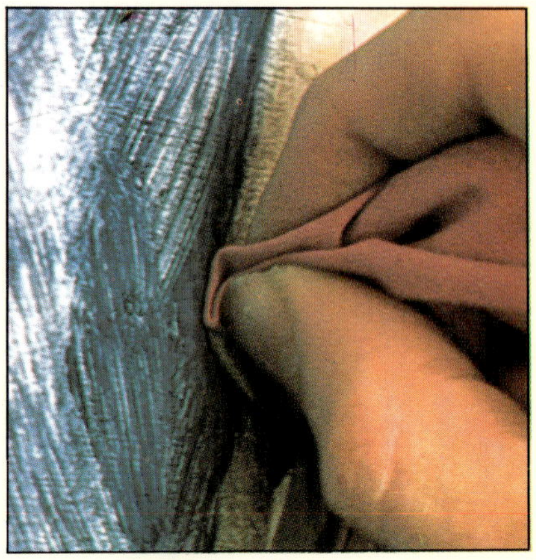

While the paint is still wet, the artist cleans up the facial area where background color has run over with a small piece of rag and turpentine.

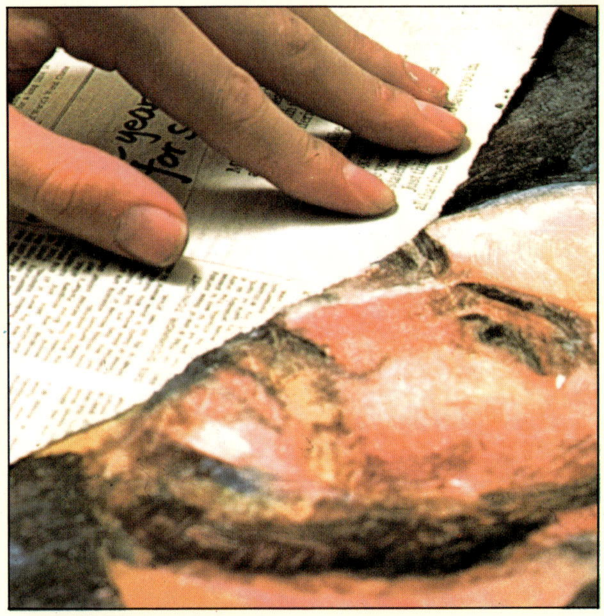

If the paint surface becomes too wet to work on, a piece of newspaper or absorbent towelling can be laid over it, lightly pressed, and lifted off. Be sure not to press too hard or to move the paper on the surface.

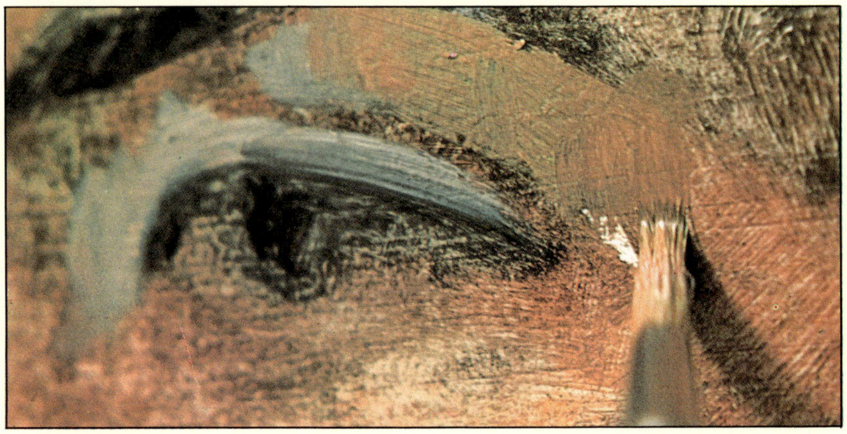

With a small brush and a middle flesh tone, the artist begins to work into the details of the eye over the dry underpainting. Note how the underpainting shows through the paint.

1. Use brown and blue to make a neutral color and outline the basic shape of the face and features with a No 3 bristle brush.

2. Start to define warm and cool color areas with flesh tones, dark yellow and brown. Strengthen the background color and cover the entire background area.

3. Spread the paint in the background and lighten highlight areas with a dry rag. Use dark colors and flesh tones in the face, using the No 3 bristle brush.

4. Paint shadows on the head and neck with dark red and work over the hair and beard with greenish-brown.

5. Build up shadows and highlights in the face and hair using small dabbing strokes to blend the colors. Darken the left side of the background.

6. Blot off the excess paint from the whole surface with a sheet of newspaper. Applying the paint more thickly, build up the dark tones.

7. Use a No 5 sable to apply highlights of light yellow and pink. Paint the jacket with a thick layer of light color.

8. Work over the whole image, blending the colors and redefining the forms. Give the shadows a slightly cooler cast with thin overlays of yellow ochre and brown.

9. Make a thin glaze of red paint, using an oil medium, and work over the flesh tones. Strengthen the highlights with thick dabs of white paint. *(continued overleaf)*

Finished picture · shadows and highlights

As a final step, the artist decided to put a scarf around the man's neck (left). This provides an interesting contrast to the face and liveliness of the image.

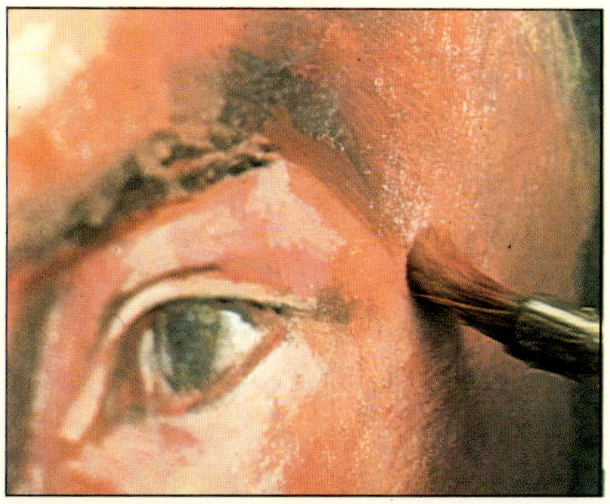

With a fine sable brush, the artist develops the shadow and highlight areas around the eye.

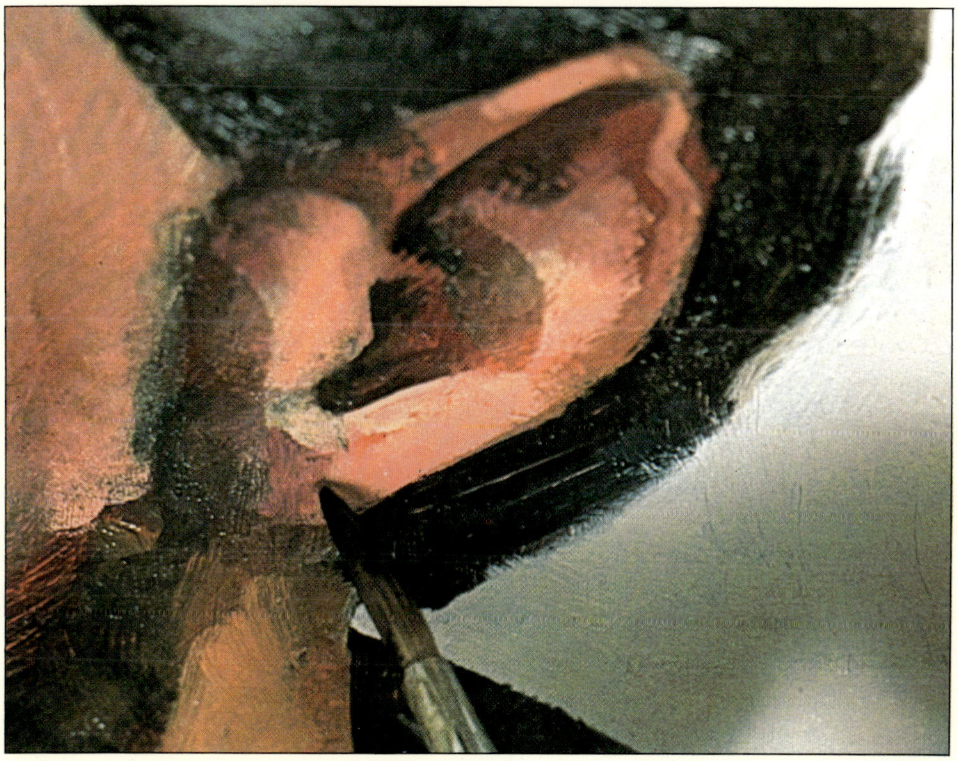

Small touches of highlight and shadow are put in with a small brush in the final stages of the painting. Here the artist defines the model's ear.

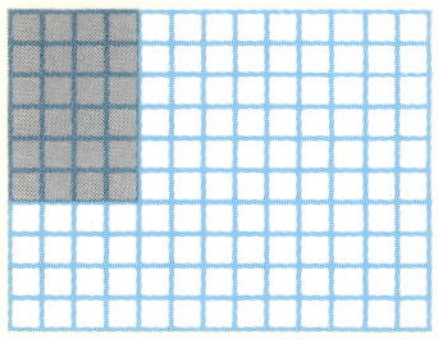

10. Lighten the color of the background, at the same time correcting the outlines.

11. Alter the tone of the whole background area, leaving a darker shadow at one side of the face.

12. Using the background color as a guide, make adjustments to the tone and color over the entire image, blending the paint with light strokes of the brush.

PAINTING A PORTRAIT in profile, as opposed to the traditional full-faced approach, can yield interesting results. When working in this way, however, there is a danger of producing a flat and predictable picture. A bare profile against a plain background can easily become simplistic and uninteresting to look at.

In this painting, the artist has avoided this in two ways. The face has been modelled with a textural and tonal complexity which overrides the simplicity of its shape and position on the canvas. The details of the hair, being the only part of the picture to incorporate fine lines of color, serve to bring the observer's eyes into the face. Curving downward and to the right, these details bring the eyes repeatedly into the subject area.

The artist has also exploited the dark blue background to heighten the lighter, warmer tones of the face and set off the profile in sharp contrast. The sitter appears to be cast in a strong, direct light, the source of which is unknown, and therefore the painting becomes more interesting to the viewer.

Materials

Surface
Prepared canvas board

Size
12in × 15in (30cm × 37.5cm)

Tools
Nos 2 and 4 flat bristle brushes
Palette
Palette knife

Colors

Black	Scarlet lake
Burnt sienna	Ultramarine
Burnt umber	White
Cadmium red medium	Yellow ochre

Mediums
Turpentine
Linseed oil

1. With a thin wash of turpentine and burnt umber, block in the shadow areas in hair and background. With a No 2 brush, establish facial features.

2. With a No 4 brush, mix a loose wash of cadmium red, umber and white and block in the red tones of the face. With yellow ochre and white, define highlight areas.

3. Mix black, white and a touch of burnt umber and put in the shadows around the eyes with the No 2 brush.

Finished picture

A profile can produce a strong, vibrant portrait as seen in the finished painting. Care must be taken to balance the bold outline of the profile with the background.

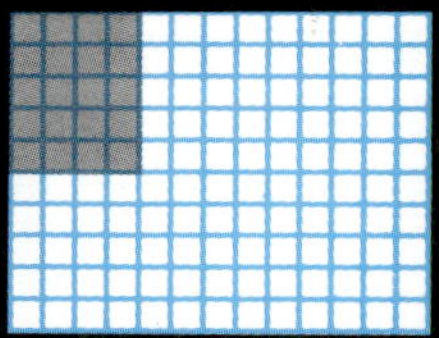

4. With white and a small amount of red, blend in warm highlights on cheek bones, forehead, and nose. Lay down color and blend with a clean, dry brush.

5. Mix umber and white and, with a No 4 brush, model in shadow areas of the chin, blending the edges into the previous layer.

6. Mix a wash of blue and black and, with a large brush, cover background area. With a small brush and white and yellow ochre, put in hair details.

A CLASSICAL technique was used to create this painting. The artist began by loosely blocking in the general warm and cool areas and building them up, constantly modifying and adjusting the tones to create a harmonious color balance. Note that the warm tones are contrasted with small touches of green, and the finished painting has an overall atmosphere of coolness.

The composition also follows classical lines, with the traditional triangle placed firmly in the centre of the picture plane. The figure is heavy and immovable and has a solidity which allows the artist to indulge in fine, delicate details within the face.

It is worth noting the various changes and alterations which took place during the painting process. Note in particular that the artist altered the tone of the background from a greenish white to a darker green, and then back again to the original color. Such a change of mind is not unusual in the painting process and it is rare for an artist to keep the first colors or shapes decided upon. The only way to find out if a color is right is to put it into the picture confidently, and then modify or change it to suit the painting as a whole, if necessary. This process of modifying and altering should take place continuously as the painting develops.

Materials

Surface
Prepared canvas board

Size
18in × 14in (45 × 35cm)

Tools
No 2 sable brush
No 3 and 5 flat bristle brush
Palette

Colors

Black	Cadmium red
Burnt umber	Cobalt blue
Cadmium green	White
Cadmium red light	Yellow ochre

Mediums
Turpentine
Polysaturated linseed oil

Finished picture · blocking in highlight areas · correcting

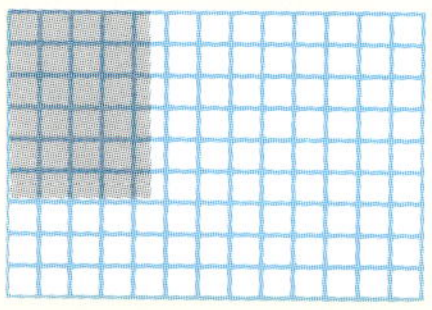

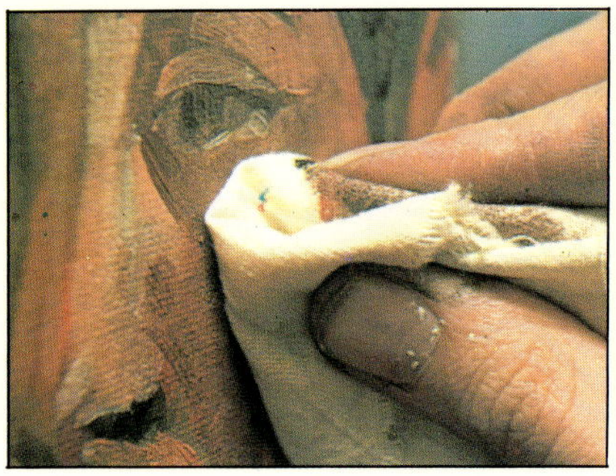

With a clean, dry rag, the artist wipes back an unwanted area. This can then be cleaned with cotton dipped in turpentine and immediately reworked.

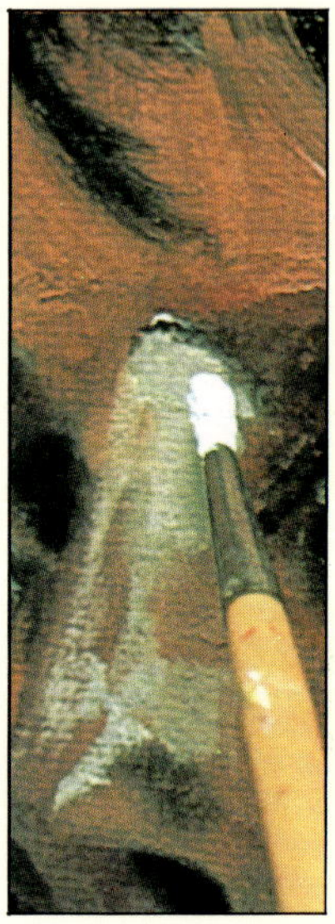

When the underpainting has dried, the artist blocks in strong highlight areas with shades of white. These areas are then toned down and modified by subsequent colors blended into the white.

1. With red, ochre and white, create general color areas of the face. Scrub in pure white around the head and draw the features in black with a No 5 brush.

2. Lighten the background area with white, black, and pale grey. With white and yellow ochre define general highlight areas of the face with a No 3 brush.

3. With cadmium red medium, block in the shirt. Using the same tone, develop warm color areas of the face, blending into the previous paint layer

4. Work back into the face with cadmium red, yellow ochre and white, painting over previous white areas and blending.

5. With white and burnt umber, work into shadow and dark detail areas. Mix cobalt blue, white, and black and block in the background with a No 5 brush.

6. With a warmer, lighter shade of white and cadmium red, blend features and details of face. Smooth out background with white and large brush.

7. With burnt umber and white, redefine planes of face with even strokes. Mix white, cadmium green and yellow ochre and thickly cover the background.

8. With a No 3 sable brush and white paint, put highlights in hair and face. Carry greenish tone of background into the scarf.

9. With the small sable brush and white, touch up highlights within the face.